Hoping for the Best
While Preparing for the Worst

Disasters, Emergencies, and the Community College

The League for Innovation in the Community College is an international organization dedicated to catalyzing the community college movement. The League hosts conferences and institutes, develops web resources, conducts research, produces publications, provides services, and leads projects and initiatives with more than 750 member colleges, 150 corporate partners, and a host of other government and nonprofit agencies in a continuing effort to make a positive difference for students and communities. Information about the League and its activities is available at www.league.org.

 This publication is available in digital form through the League's iStream, www.league.org/istream.

Contents

Acknowledgements

The stories compiled in this book relay the experiences of our colleagues in community colleges across the country who have been through devastating storms and other extraordinary situations. When we asked our friends to share their stories, we knew we were also asking them to relive disturbing, even painful moments in their own lives and in the lives of their institutions. We are grateful to all of the authors for their contributions, and to the authors' many colleagues whose memories were tapped as they were asked to assist in the retelling of events. Many of the situations described in the following pages were unavoidable, but the great lesson learned is that with thorough planning, preparation, and practice, the damages to property, and more important, to lives, can be diminished.

Thanks especially to Bob Romine of the Alabama College System for providing information about the Alabama evacuation plan. Special thanks also go to Fawn Belone, Tracy Churchill, and our colleagues on the League staff for their assistance in this project. In particular, we are especially grateful to Cynthia Wilson, Vice President for Learning and Research, League for Innovation, whose talent, dedication, and editing skills were invaluable for "fixing the roof when the sun was shining."

Alice W. Villadsen
Gerardo E. de los Santos

Foreword

Long before September 11, community colleges were the leaders in emergency response and emergency prevention training. Chances are the police officer who patrols your neighborhood, the firefighter who teaches fire safety to your children, and the nurse or emergency medical technician who tends your illnesses or injuries were trained at your local community college. Eighty percent of first responders are trained at a community college.

However, September 11 required community colleges to expand their programs to address the need for enhanced training for communities' response systems. Fields critical to homeland security – law enforcement and public safety, health care, information technology and cyber security, biotechnology and community services – are fields that depend on community colleges to prepare their professionals. Thus, this compilation of emergency response stories comes from people who know their business. Community colleges have the unique perspective and a long history of knowing the emergency response textbook answer and the real-life challenges of emergency responses. And because community colleges, in many ways, mirror the community – in our people and our operations – emergency management at community colleges contains lessons for other organizations and municipalities. Readers will find valuable takeaways in the case studies presented here.

Many of the colleges represented in this book are well known for their innovation and commitment to quality programming. The Dallas County Community College District, Miami Dade College, St. Louis Community College, and Santa Fe Community College hold seats, along with Monroe Community College, on the board of the League for Innovation in the Community College. I have visited each of these colleges, know their presidents, and can personally attest to their commitment to and track record for excellence and innovation. With the other fine colleges in this collection, their examples of emergency responses are worthy of attention.

The combination in this collection of knowledge, experience, and innovation gives all of us a valuable learning tool. However, I encourage you to go beyond the words on these pages: ask questions, visit and engage a community college in the homeland security and public safety discussion. Community colleges across this country are collaborative institutions; we welcome opportunities to share what we know and to learn from others.

When it comes to homeland security and public safety, our nation depends upon community colleges to provide the best possible training. Securing our country is a challenge community colleges embrace with enthusiasm and pride.

R. Thomas Flynn, President
Monroe Community College
Rochester, New York

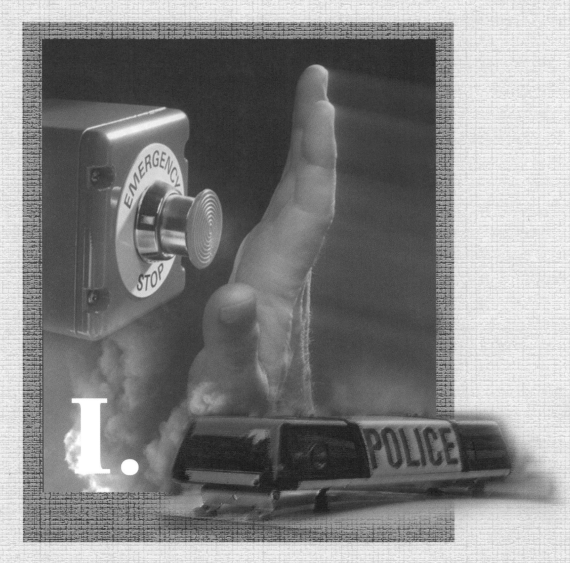

I.

Disaster Preparedness and the Community College

Chapter 1

Community Colleges Preparing for Emergencies and Disasters: A Review of Research and Resources

Gerardo E. de los Santos

Disaster Preparednes and the Community College

September 11, Hurricanes Katrina, Rita, and Ivan, the SARS outbreak, the anthrax threats, and the pandemic flu are all recent events that have caused community colleges to re-examine preparedness plans and training for emergencies, disasters, and terrorism. Most leaders and policy

fields of law enforcement and public safety, health care, information technology and cyber security, biotechnology, hazardous materials, and community service all leverage community colleges. From Monroe Community College's public safety training facility, which includes two 737 aircraft

"The time to repair the roof is when the sun is shining."

John F. Kennedy

makers recognize that a key to readiness is targeted education and training, both in terms of improving and expanding existing delivery and creating new high-stakes training focused on disaster preparedness, infrastructure recovery, and business continuity (Flynn et al., 2003). As community college leaders, we need, when the sun is shining, to take the important steps to repair the roof of emergency and disaster preparedness.

In the U.S. alone, more than 1,100 community and technical colleges serve more than 10 million students annually with a comprehensive array of educational programs targeted to meet the education and training needs of their communities (Flynn et al., 2003). More germane is the fact that community colleges are arguably the linchpin and often unheralded emergency, disaster, and homeland security training providers. Indeed, many of the heroes of September 11 and Hurricanes Rita, Katrina, and Ivan were our former students. The

burn simulators at its state-of-the-art facility, to Miami-Dade College's cyber security program, to Kirkwood Community College's hazardous materials and mass fatalities training center, to the Maricopa Community Colleges National Community College Center for Civic Engagement, the reach and scope of the American community college training capacity is stunning. In short, community and technical colleges are central to the discussion when exploring emergency, disaster, and terror preparedness (Flynn et al., 2003).

The League for Innovation in the Community College presents this book as a resource for prompting community college discussions focused on disaster and emergency preparedness. The book begins, in this chapter, with a review of research and resources on emergency, disaster, and terror planning for public institutions. This chapter ends with a list of resources available to community colleges as they consider potential scenarios and

Disaster Preparedness and the Community College

responses. In the second chapter, Alice W. Villadsen synthesizes the collective wisdom of contributors and other community college leaders who have seen their institutions through emergency and disaster situations. In Chapters 3 through 7, leaders from colleges that have experienced hurricane and tornado devastation share their stories, including lessons learned, from planning for anticipated storms to surviving tempests, to cleaning up and rebuilding campuses, communities, and lives in the aftermath. Chapters 8, 9, and 10 present personal perspectives: a president, administrator in charge,

FROM FIRST-RESPONDER TRAINING TO COMPREHENSIVE EMERGENCY AND DISASTER PREPAREDNESS PROGRAMS

Often based on community need and likelihood of emergency, many community and technical colleges have developed guidelines for emergencies and natural disasters, which often include events such as tornadoes, earthquakes, floods, bomb threats and searches, power outages, and fires. In addition, many community colleges have been long-time providers of training for first responders,

Many community and technical colleges have developed guidelines for emergencies and natural disasters.

and police chief sharing their experiences and views following an anthrax scare on campus; a president dealing with the murder of a colleague on campus; and a communications professional handling an unexplained death on campus. The final two chapters present, respectively, a state plan for using community college facilities as emergency shelters and one college's process for developing emergency and disaster preparedness plans.

Although many of the chapters in this book focus on specific weather-related disasters and human-made emergency situations, many emergency and disaster preparedness and training programs in community colleges address a much broader range of incidents that are discussed in this initial chapter. This chapter also presents a review of research and resources in the broad context of the federal government and public institutions as they relate to community and technical colleges. The second chapter presents a more thorough examination of specific community college emergency and disaster experiences and shares practical advice to those who must plan for and provide leadership through a number of emergencies that affect community colleges.

and they house and operate emergency and disaster preparedness training and institutes. Community college training for first responders includes public safety and law enforcement, as well as training in the areas of agroterror and biosecurity, health care, biotechnology, cyber security, hazardous materials, mass fatalities, disaster recovery, international relations, language training, community awareness and engagement, and more. What is remarkable is the range and sophistication of training programs already in place and the enormity of the role two-year colleges already play in maintaining community preparedness, safety, and security (Flynn et al., 2003).

While a number of community and technical colleges provide first-responder training for firefighters, EMTs, and police officers, they are expanding their emergency, disaster, and terror preparedness programs and training. For example, Monroe Community College in Rochester, New York, operates the Public Safety Training Facility dedicated to the mission of providing "best-in-class, cost-effective training to first responders, public officials, businesspeople, safety professionals, health-care providers, and all citizens who may play a role in an emergency." This comprehensive training facility includes paramedic training, an emergency services program, the Homeland Security Management Institute, the Northeast Fire Training Center, security officer training, law enforcement recruit training, and in-service law enforcement training, all focused not only on minimizing risk, but also providing critical knowledge of response, prevention, and operational management (www.monroecc.edu/depts/pstc).

Kirkwood Community College in Cedar Rapids, Iowa, also provides a wide range of emergency and disaster training. Kirkwood operates the Community Training and Response Center, which houses the Environmental Technology Center, the National Mass Fatalities Institute, the Hazardous Materials Training and Research Institute, the AgTerror Preparedness Center, and the Midwest OSHA Education Center – all managed by Kirkwood Community College's Environmental Health, Safety, and Security Department – and the Linn County Emergency Management Agency (www.hmtri.org).

TYPES OF EMERGENCIES AND DISASTERS

While community and technical colleges encounter specific types of emergencies and incidents such as accidents, crimes, or medical emergencies, and community health issues relative to region, proximity, or role in their respective communities, the Federal Emergency Management Agency (FEMA) lists emergency and disaster events as follows: hurricanes, fires or wildfires, earthquakes, terrorism, floods, tornadoes, severe weather, landslides, nuclear power plant emergencies, tsunamis, volcanoes, thunderstorms, and dam failures (FEMA, 2007, www.fema.gov/hazard/types.shtm). Other emergencies or disasters for which community colleges provide training and community service include, but are not limited to, hazardous substance spills, technology, telecommunications and information services failure, utility failure, and pandemic influenza.

FEMA (2007) also describes local, state, and federal government and volunteer agency response and recovery roles and responsibilities in the face of an emergency or disaster:

- First response to a disaster is the job of local government's emergency services with help from nearby municipalities, the state, and volunteer agencies. In a catastrophic disaster, and if the governor requests, federal resources can be mobilized through FEMA for search and rescue, electrical power, food, water, shelter, and other basic human needs.

- It is the long-term recovery phase of disaster that places the most severe financial strain on a local or state government. Damage to public facilities and infrastructure, often not insured, can overwhelm even a large city.

- A governor's request for a major disaster declaration could mean an infusion of federal funds, but the governor must also commit significant state funds and resources for recovery efforts.

- A major disaster could result from a hurricane, earthquake, flood, tornado, or major fire that the president determines warrants supplemental federal aid. The event must be clearly more than state or local governments can handle alone. If declared, funding comes from the President's Disaster Relief Fund, which is managed by FEMA, and disaster aid programs of other participating federal agencies.

- A presidential major disaster declaration puts into motion long-term federal recovery programs, some of which are matched by state programs, and designed to help disaster victims, businesses, and public entities.

- An emergency declaration is more limited in scope and without the long-term federal recovery programs of a major disaster declaration. Generally, federal assistance and funding are provided to meet a specific emergency need or to help prevent a major disaster from occurring. (www.fema.gov/hazard/types.shtm)

Disaster Preparedness and the Community College

A major disaster declaration usually follows these steps:

- Local government responds, supplemented by neighboring communities and volunteer agencies. If overwhelmed, turn to the state for assistance.

- The state responds with state resources, such as the National Guard and state agencies.

- Damage assessment by local, state, federal, and volunteer organizations determines losses and recovery needs.

- A major disaster declaration is requested by the governor, based on the damage assessment, and an agreement to commit state funds and resources to the long-term recovery.

- FEMA evaluates the request and recommends action to the White House based on the disaster, the local community, and the state's ability to recover.

- The president approves the request or FEMA informs the governor it has been denied. This decision process could take a few hours or several weeks depending on the nature of the disaster. (FEMA, 2007, www.fema.gov/hazard/dproc.shtm)

your business, disrupt operations, cause physical or environmental damage, or threaten the facility's financial standing or public image" (www.fema.gov/hazard/types.shtm).

With the disasters of September 11 and Hurricanes Katrina, Rita, and Ivan fresh in memory, community colleges are under the necessary pressure to ensure they are prepared for an increasing number of possible emergency incidents or natural disasters. Many community colleges throughout the country have put into place emergency and disaster preparedness plans and guidelines, which serve as a set of shared procedures intended to avoid or recover from disasters. Lyall (1993) defines a disaster plan as "a document which describes the procedures devised to prevent and prepare for disasters, and those proposed to respond to and recover from disasters when they occur" (¶2). Lyall (1993) also poses that a comprehensive disaster plan consists of smaller, independent, interrelated plans to deal with the "before, during, and after" (¶3) phases of a disaster or emergency situation. These phases and their corresponding plans range from preventive and preparedness plans in operation prior to the disaster situation, to response plans that are enacted during the event, and recovery plans that are adaptable to the needs of various incidents that may occur.

Community colleges are under the necessary pressure to ensure they are prepared for an increasing number of possible emergency incidents or natural disasters.

DEFINING EMERGENCY AND DISASTER PLANNING

According to the Federal Emergency Management Agency (2007), an emergency is defined as "any unplanned event that can cause deaths or significant injuries to employees, customers, or the public; or that can shut down

Jones (2000) describes four phases of disaster planning as (1) preparedness, or preparing to handle an emergency, which incorporates plans or preparations to save lives and help response-and-rescue operation; (2) response, or responding safely to an emergency, which addresses actions taken to save lives and prevent further property damage in a disaster or emergency situation; (3) recovery, or recovering from an emergency, which includes those actions taken to return to a normal or an even safer situation following emergency; and (4) mitigation, or preventing future emergencies or minimizing their effects, which includes any activities that prevent an emergency, reduce the chance of an emergency happening, or reduce the damaging affects of unavoidable emergencies.

INFRASTRUCTURE RECOVERY PLANNING AND BUSINESS CONTINUITY

Whether or not we fully realize it, everyone on our college campuses relies on information technology. Therefore, infrastructure recovery, which

change and service management, and classrooms. Critical questions also need to guide the development of recovery planning:

1. What are your recovery time and recovery point objectives?
2. What are your organizational requirements?
3. What are your business drivers?
4. What is your budget?
5. Do you have the resources to implement and maintain the solution? (Baker and Whorton, 2005).

Another critical aspect of infrastructure recovery planning is identifying major information technology

Colleges need to focus disaster preparedness plans on business continuity rather than recovery.

entails the technological aspect of business continuity planning, is among the critical priorities in disaster planning. Infrastructure recovery involves the advance planning and preparations necessary to minimize loss and ensure continuity of the critical business function of an organization in the event of disaster (www.drii.org). The intended outcome of infrastructure recovery is to regain the activities that restore the institution to an acceptable condition after suffering from a disaster (Yanosky, 2006).

In preparing an infrastructure recovery plan, a myriad of questions needs to be considered. According to Baker and Whorton (2005), the key issues that surround infrastructure recovery include threats, budget, growing data volume, and resources. Swartz (2006) characterizes commonly identified areas of information technology risk and points of failure as the data center, telecommunications, the network and ISP, data, security, power and cooling,

vulnerabilities such as loss of or damage to buildings housing computer rooms; loss of the building housing the central network hub, cutting off access to the rest of campus; loss of the building housing the internet connection; and damage to administrative or web servers (Maltz and Kreager, 2003).

BUSINESS CONTINUITY: TAKING DISASTER RECOVERY TO THE NEXT LEVEL

Colleges need to focus disaster preparedness plans on business continuity rather than recovery (Swartz, 2006), and Yanosky (2006) defines business continuity as the institution's ability to maintain or restore its business and academic services when some circumstance threatens or disrupts normal operations. Yanosky (2006) further explains that business continuity encompasses disaster recovery – the

Disaster Preparedness and the Community College

activities that restore the institution to an acceptable condition after suffering a disaster – and also includes activities such as risk and impact assessment, prioritization of business processes, and restoring operations to a "new normal" after an event.

Basic characteristics of business continuity also include an emphasis on front-end service delivery, not back-end infrastructure; a holistic, collaborative, enterprisewide approach; a focus on postrecovery change; and an understanding that information technology supports business continuity, yet cannot "deliver" it (Yanosky, 2006).

According to Swartz (2006), a solid continuity plan must include three priorities:

1. Continuity of operations needs to be built into the architecture of the plan and culture of the institution from the bottom up.

2. If you live and use the plan day to day, then you are more familiar with it when disaster hits.

3. Business continuity at a comprehensive local level is essential to enable information technology to deliver the sustainability of data and information services.

Business continuity and disaster recovery planning are not to be confused with loss prevention planning, which comprises regularly scheduled activities such as backups, system authentication and authorization (security), virus scanning, and system usage monitoring (Michigan State University, 2001).

yet are certainly not limited to (1) services to adult survivors and victims' families, which may include mental health professionals, mass casualty personnel, a compassion center, critical incident stress management, crisis counseling, and death notification teams; (2) services to children, which may include crisis counseling, YMCA services, child specialists, and a compassion center; (3) services to first-response teams and rescue-and-recovery workers, which may include mental health services and disaster mental health services for spouses and families of first-response and rescue-and-recovery teams, (4) mental health and clergy response, which may include on- and off-site mental health professionals, psychologists, and clergy, and (5) transition from immediate to long-term disaster mental health services, which may include crisis counseling, outreach and public information, support groups, and training and consultation (Task Force, 1997).

HOPING FOR THE BEST WHILE PREPARING FOR THE WORST

Community colleges are inherently optimistic institutions. In our optimism, we invite everyone to come through our open doors, and we offer a multitude of services to help those who accept the invitation achieve their educational and career goals. In our optimism, we hope for the best for our students, for our communities, for ourselves. We do not imagine, however, that we or our students will achieve the best without careful planning and

The key to readiness is targeted education and training.

MENTAL HEALTH RESPONSE SERVICES

Another important aspect of disaster preparedness surrounds mental health response services that may be required for various people involved in the disaster. These services may include,

concentrated effort. In thinking about disaster and emergency preparedness, we need not abandon our optimism. We can certainly hope for the best, but as we have been reminded all too frequently in recent years, we must also prepare for the disaster and emergency situations that may come our way. The key to readiness is targeted education and training, as well as shared understanding of disaster preparedness, infrastructure recovery, and business continuity (Flynn et al., 2003). Community and technical college leaders are re-examining preparedness plans and training efforts for emergencies, disasters, and terrorism, and are taking the necessary steps to best position their institutions and communities in the event of a disaster.

REFERENCES

Baker, K., and Whorton, B. (2005). *Preparing for Disaster: How to Protect Your Infrastructure*. Vernon Hills, IL: CDW-G. Accessed at www.educause.edu/ir/library/powerpoint/SER0502.pps.

Disaster Recovery Institute International. (2006). The Institute for Continuity Management. Accessed at www.drii.org.

Flynn, R.T., Milliron, M.D., de los Santos, G.E., and Miles, C.L. (2003 July). Homeland Security and the Community College: A Vibrant Present and Vital Future. *Leadership Abstracts 16:7*. Phoenix: League for Innovation in the Community College.

Jones, W.M. (2000 March). Trial by Tornado. One Records Facility's Response to a Devastating Tornado Demonstrates the Necessity of a Solid Disaster Recovery Plan. *Infopro 2:1*, 37-39.

Kirkwood Community College. (2007). Community Training and Response Center. Accessed at www.hmtri.org.

Lyall, J.(1993). Disaster Planning for Libraries and Archives: Understanding the Essential Issues. Paper presented at and published in the proceedings (pp. 103-112) of the *Pan-African Conference on the Preservation and Conservation of Library and Archival Materials*, Nairobi, Kenya: June 21-25, 1993. Accessed at www.nla.gov.au/nla/staffpaper/lyall1.html.

Maltz, L., and Kreager, G. (2003). Disaster Recovery Planning: Because It's Time. New York, NY, and Waltham, MA: Columbia University and Bentley College. Accessed at www.educause.edu/ir/library/powerpoint/NCP0327.pps.

Michigan State University. (2001). Unit Guide to Disaster Recovery Planning.

Monroe Community College. (2007). Homeland Security Management Institute. Accessed at www.monroecc.edu/depts/pstc.

Swartz, D. (2006). Going Beyond Recovery to Continuity: Lessons Learned. George Washington University. Accessed at www.gwu.edu/~galert/.

Task Force on the Mental Health Response to the Oklahoma City Bombing. (1997). Final Report. Washington, DC: American Psychological Association.

United States Department of Homeland Security. Federal Emergency Management Agency. (2007). Disaster Information. The Disaster Process and Disaster Aid Programs. Accessed at www.fema.gov/hazard/dproc.shtm.

United States Department of Homeland Security. Federal Emergency Management Agency. (2007). Disaster Information. Types of Disasters. Accessed at www.fema.gov/hazard/types.shtm.

Yanosky, R. (2006) Tracking the Storm: Higher Education IT Readiness for Business Continuity. Presentation at the Fifth Annual ECAR/HP Summer Symposium for Higher Education IT Executives, June 28-30, 2006, Coronado, CA. Accessed at www.educause.edu/content.asp?page_id=666&ID=ECR0604&bhcp=1.

Gerardo E. de los Santos is President and CEO of the League for Innovation in the Community College.

Selected Resources

UNITED STATES GOVERNMENT RESOURCES

United States Department of Commerce, www.commerce.gov

- National Oceanic and Atmospheric Administration, www.noaa.gov
- National Weather Service, www.nws.noaa.gov
- National Hurricane Center, Hurricane Preparedness www.nhc.noaa.gov/HAW2/english/disaster_prevention.shtml

United States Department of Health and Human Services

- National Disaster Medical System, http://ndms.dhhs.gov

United States Department of Homeland Security, www.dhs.gov/index.shtm

- Federal Emergency Management Agency, www.fema.gov.
- United States Department of Homeland Security, Ready.gov, www.ready.gov

United States Department of Labor, www.dol.gov

- Incident Command System, Occupational Safety and Health Administration, www.osha.gov/SLTC/etools/ics/

United States National Library of Medicine and the National Institutes of Health, www.nlm.nih.gov

- MedlinePlus, http://medlineplus.gov
- Disaster Preparation and Recovery, www.nlm.nih.gov/medlineplus/disasterpreparationandrecovery.html

OTHER NATIONAL ORGANIZATION RESOURCES

American Red Cross, www.redcross.org

- Disaster Services, www.redcross.org/services/disaster/0,1082,0_500_,00.html
- www.prepare.org

The Disaster Preparedness and Emergency Response Association (DERA), www.disasters.org

National Center for Disaster Preparedness, Columbia University Mailman School of Public Health, www.ncdp.mailman.columbia.edu/

National Clearinghouse for Educational Facilities, www.edfacilities.org

- Resource Lists. Disaster Preparedness and Response for Schools www.edfacilities.org/rl/disaster.cfm

National Fire Service Incident Management System Consortium, www.ims-consortium.org

National Incident Management System Online, www.nimsonline.com

Chapter 2

Collective Wisdom

Alice W. Villadsen

Disaster Preparedness and the Community College

Within this chapter, the author has collected and distilled advice and best practices from the community college disaster and emergency stories that make up the remainder of this book. The intent is to provide practical advice to those who must plan and provide leadership through any number of emergencies that affect community colleges. The following collective wisdom comes from the hard lessons of experience: Hurricanes Ivan and Katrina, tornadoes, campus incidents of physical violence or threats of such, and other natural and human-made disasters. At times, the emergency required the college to evacuate; in others, students, faculty, and staff took shelter in campus buildings against severe weather or violence; in still others, the college was required to keep all students and employees in place, in a lock-down mode. In every case, a guiding principle reported by chapter authors, regardless of the emergency situation, was to reopen the college as soon as possible so that students and staff could resume some semblance of normalcy and the work of educating students could continue.

DISASTER PLANS

The necessity for community colleges to have emergency and disaster plans has long been understood by those in positions of college leadership. Since September 11, emergency procedures and disaster preparation plans have become increasingly detailed and complex. Within this book is one college's story of coming into compliance with new federal regulations mandated

for all colleges. The Monroe Community College Emergency Management Plan is based upon the new presidential directive, issued in 2003 and mandated for all federal response organizations. It is called the National Incident Management System. All readers are urged to study the information included in Chapter 12, "Creating and Sustaining a Campus Emergency Management Plan that Works," by R. Thomas Flynn, president, and Lee E. Struble, director of public safety, at Monroe. Access to Monroe's fine work and all related guidelines are included within the chapter. However, this chapter contains advice for college leaders from the stories of actual disaster that have been selected for inclusion in this book.

The plan itself must be broad enough to cover any number of possible disasters, flexible enough to include responses to the unexpected, and clear enough to be understood at the college not only by first responders and college leaders, but also by every faculty member, student, and staff person. Typically, plans will include weather-related emergencies such as hurricanes, tornadoes, damaging hail, ice storms, floods, earthquakes, and mud slides; human-made emergency situations such as bombs and bomb threats, gun violence, explosions, chemical or radiation spills and leaks, utility failures, elevator malfunctions, and outbreaks of communicable diseases or pandemics; and often more common possibilities such as peaceful or violent demonstrations on campus and sudden illnesses like cardiac/vascular emergencies and seizures. The strong, dynamic plan must be tested and retested. Although not easily accomplished and sometimes disruptive, practice drills must be a part of the plan, including both actual drills and tabletop scenarios for the emergency leadership team. The president must have the tenacity to insist that the plan be tested and supported. The plan must be evaluated regularly so that it changes as a result of practice drills and actual emergency experiences. Debriefings after practice drills have proved to be effective in plan improvements.

Any plan must include the types of disasters and the appropriate responses for each, whether evacuation or lock-down of the college, or retreat to safer locations; key employees and chain of command for the emergency; state-of-emergency rules and regulations; a communication plan; and a recovery plan. Of course, if the college is open in

A second, detailed plan is written and distributed to the key college leaders, emergency team members, police and maintenance staff, information technology officers, and others like building coordinators. The plan is often also available online.

Those who have experienced emergencies requiring implementation of the disaster plan say that it is essential that all college employees responsible for any part of the plan's success, and a second backup employee in case of absence of the key employee, (1) be identified early; (2) have office, home, and cell telephone numbers gathered and included; (3) be listed in all appropriate publications and on wallet cards for all employees' information; and (4) be trained to complete the tasks for which they are assigned. Means for the emergency team to communicate

> *Means for the emergency team to communicate with each other and the college must be provided, with battery-powered devices often the most fail-safe method.*

the evening and on weekends, the plan must include specifics for students and staff to follow at those times. Depending upon the size and complexity of the organization, several plans may be required for sufficient detail to be available on multiple sites or in scattered college buildings. For Miami Dade College, administrators determined three priorities within their plan, beyond personal safety: the physical plant, business operations, and information technology resources.

For many colleges, an answer to having a plan that is both complete enough to provide appropriate detail and simple enough to be understood by all is to provide a simplified plan for posting via web, voice messages, and message boards and for distribution to students, to faculty and staff who have no assigned responsibility within the emergency plan, and for the public.

with each other and the college must be provided, with battery-powered devices often the most fail-safe method. Cell phones with remote area codes or satellite phones are alternatives for communications as well. With many weather-related emergencies, local cell phones become inoperative because of downed cell towers. As emergencies unfold, some colleges report the usefulness of telephone conference bridging capabilities for team communication and communication with outside agencies.

An organizational structure that has worked well is the appointment of building and college site coordinators. These individuals, usually volunteers, are trained in their duties, are provided with a means of communication and a vest or hat to identify themselves as coordinators during an emergency, and sometimes are given first aid training and materials. During practice of evacuation, relocations, or lock-downs, volunteers' work and reports to the administration about the practice run are critical to the operations of the emergency plan. They also serve to ensure that

Prior to any emergency situation, the wise college also has arranged for the off-site backup of critical college data, has ensured that its own information technology equipment is as safe as

Presidents who have dealt with significant college emergencies report that setting direction and tone are crucial elements of crisis leadership.

buildings are clear or that normal operations have resumed once the crisis is over. Through their careful work during the crisis, security and maintenance staff members can provide quick inspections to report damage, injury, or other vital information about a location.

Prior to any emergency situation, the administration should have determined which employees must remain on duty during the emergency if the college is evacuated. A location for emergency team headquarters needs to be determined and noted within the plan. The availability of a second meeting place in case the primary one is destroyed or unavailable is a good precaution and was essential for Delgado with Hurricane Katrina and Volunteer State with its tornado.

Although typically not a part of the disaster plan itself, the availability of a rainy-day fund at the college has proved hugely important in massive disasters. Although insurance, state and federal funds, and donations are mentioned as crucial in repair and renovation of college structures, the immediate need for cash for emergency repairs is great. In Tennessee, the state system provides previously contracted services for such emergencies. At Miami Dade, prearranged agreements with repair services eliminated the delays that purchase orders and state bids create for a college in crisis.

possible, located away from ground floor flooding possibilities, and has established a means whereby the college's website and online services can be continued. Prior study and preparation for working with crucial agencies like FEMA or state emergency management operations can increase the likelihood of smooth relationships and early aid to the college.

THE ROLE OF THE PRESIDENT

Presidential responsibility and presidential leadership are never more important than when disaster strikes a college. However, prior to any crisis, a wise president has insisted upon a workable and tested emergency plan and has conducted serious drills regardless of lack of enthusiasm from faculty and staff about the disruption that such practice usually entails. The president has sent strong messages to the college and its students about emergency preparations when, for example, weather bulletins predict hurricanes, tornadoes, or other severe weather conditions, or at the beginning of storm seasons. The president has also adopted a conservative approach by making closing decisions as early as possible and always maintaining an awareness of recommendations from weather services and state and local emergency managers. When away from the college, the president always ensures that a second in command is named and that key members of the college leadership team know who is in charge at all times.

Presidents assume direct leadership during the crisis, and should. Presidents who have dealt with significant college emergencies report that setting direction and tone are crucial elements of crisis leadership. Decisions often must be made quickly and without the usual consultation; and the president may need to exhibit a more demanding demeanor and may need to centralize power within a small leadership team or the emergency response team. Having a clear state-of-emergency operational manual aids the college when leadership is fragmented and sometimes simply not available in its usual context. Therefore, the strong role and visibility of the president fulfill college and community expectations. Long hours, often for weeks at a time, result from the demands of some emergency situations, so conscientiousness, resiliency, and availability are crucial. The president's visibility can comfort the college in crisis. Often the "face of the emergency" with media, the president becomes the steady, strong advocate for

that normalcy will return, and spokespersons for the college's grief.

THE EMERGENCY RESPONSE TEAM

Emergency response teams are usually the individuals at the college who have been involved in establishing the plan, rehearsing and revising the plan, and implementing the plan when an emergency occurs. Preparation and practice are the two necessary ingredients for successful emergency management teams. The teams are often made up of the president, who typically calls the team into action; other main administrators; the head of college security; the head of buildings, grounds, and maintenance; the public information officer; and the college nurse or other health professional or first responders. Each college develops its team to represent key areas of responsibility and location. Identified by name in the emergency plan and listed with appropriate location information and numbers, these individuals are usually given special communication devices and access, safety equipment, and identification tags or special

Preparation and practice are the two necessary ingredients for successful emergency management teams.

the college. He or she sets the agenda and prioritizes issues that must be addressed, whether it is payment for college employees while the college is closed, refunds for students outside of usual policy, limiting access to all or parts of the college, or the determination of dates for reopening the college. Of course, the emotional stability to maintain calm control amid chaos and havoc is a seldom practiced but important ability during the emergency.

Following the immediate situation, presidents report that they have assumed roles as comforters to affected employees and students, reassurers to all

clothing. As previously mentioned, building and site coordinators are an excellent means whereby the team can ensure that all areas of the college are notified with emergency information and someone is checking that procedures are being followed. The plan itself usually indicates each team member's responsibility, the location of team headquarters and an alternate site, and the person who has responsibility for communicating with the college and media outlets. Finally, the emergency team typically assumes responsibility for storm assessments, sometimes taking immediate pictures and videos of damage. Team training and practice is ongoing, and usually a reappointment process occurs annually.

FIRST TASKS

Common first tasks after emergencies at colleges differ depending on the crisis. However, all agree that with college damage from storms, earthquakes, fires, and such catastrophes, the following actions become paramount:

- Determine the safety of individuals on campus and conduct them to appropriate aid.

- Verify the status of facilities and vehicles, implement temporary repair processes to prevent further damage, and secure buildings.

- Confirm central administrative spaces, locate and consolidate team and primary college leadership, and prioritize most critical needs.

- Implement the communications plan.

- Restore information technology, including websites and student and administrative systems.

- When possible, set a reopening date, reopen unaffected portions of the college, and develop a plan to move classes to appropriate sites.

and employees, and on-campus short-term housing and food for those whose homes have been damaged or destroyed. When the college itself becomes a refuge for members of local communities, bedding, cots, showers, and hygiene items are required. The Alabama State Plan (see Chapter 11) provides for the community college system to be shelter sites for residents, especially those affected by hurricanes in Baldwin, Mobile, and other southern Alabama counties. This innovative plan includes many suggestions for colleges needing to become shelter sites.

COMMUNITY PARTNERS

The long tradition of community colleges functioning as a seamless extension of the local service area can provide a set of partners that are crucial during emergencies. Pre-existing cooperative relationships between the college and certain partners are logical: local emergency operations and services, the Red Cross, the National Guard, sheriffs' departments, local police units, fire departments, hospitals, utility companies, information technology service contractors, other college vendors, contractors, and builders. Good working relationships with local media outlets are

Good working relationships with local media outlets are crucial.

- Inform state agencies of any policy changes necessary to reopen – e.g., restricted schedules; student refunds; employee pay, vacation, and leave – and inform accreditation agencies and federal and state offices as appropriate.

- Provide counseling and other services for employees and students affected by the crisis.

In cases of significant damage, some colleges have provided transportation for students and staff members, short-term grants and loans for students

crucial, providing direct access to external communications options to the college's public relations director.

Cities and counties, state and federal government agencies, and elected officials can prove extremely beneficial as the college attempts to deal with slow bureaucracies and red tape. Lee College in Texas found the Volunteer Center to be the perfect partner as the college set up distribution centers for those evacuees affected by Hurricanes

Disaster Preparedness and the Community College

Katrina and Rita. Pensacola Junior College found a relationship between the college police and local restaurants provided both good food for those sheltering on campus and a means for the restaurants to empty pantries and refrigerators of food that would otherwise spoil from lack of electricity. A local bus service was available to transport stranded students and employees to their homes thanks to a prior relationship that the college had with the public transportation organization.

Finally, a strong partnership with system and state governing agencies is almost always required when a college suffers through a significant emergency situation. The colleges reported that state attendance regulations had to be temporarily lifted or eased; tuition reimbursement and cut-off dates were changed; state and local regulations affecting payment for employees had to be altered; the usual bid process was abandoned; and Pell transfers were allowed. Colleges found that their state organizations became supportive friends, and solutions were found within the existing bureaucracies to benefit students.

COMMUNICATIONS AND INFORMATION TECHNOLOGY

All colleges report that the most difficult challenge, the problem most resistant to logical planning, is the development and implementation of a successful communications plan. Often because of the elimination of trusted services during, and because of, the emergency situation, telephones and computers fail. How can a telephone tree work if cell phone towers and land lines are out? How can students be informed of reopening dates and critical financial aid information if the mainframe is under water? How can direct payment of employee payroll happen when the administrative system is inoperative?

The recommendations listed on this page come from institutions that have experienced a devastating emergency, and include actions colleges can take as they seek solutions to the complexity of maintaining communications and operations with students, employees, and the public.

RECOMMENDED ACTIONS PRIOR TO ANY EMERGENCY SITUATION

- Locate crucial hardware – information technology and voice/data communications infrastructure including routers, switches, and hubs – in a safe place, certainly not in a basement or on the ground floor.

- Find a partner for system redundancy, perhaps another community college, distant enough from your college to provide a secondary system that can be accessed in case of an emergency.

- Store duplicate critical data off site. Partner to provide a secondary website the college can use.

- Prior to an approaching storm, train all faculty and staff to disengage computers and other technology, get portable equipment off the floor and consider covering it with waterproof materials.

- Do not rely on cell phones as the primary means of communication. If cell phones are used, be sure that your emergency team members have secondary cell numbers from other prefixes and that those second numbers are listed. Consider satellite phones or, more simply, battery-operated radios for the emergency team members and building or site coordinators. Communicating during and after the emergency is critical.

- Remote access for technicians to the information technology infrastructure can be a means whereby repair or rerouting can occur on the system by individuals away from the campus.

- Many colleges are returning to older, lower technologies like intercom systems or bells for quick campus communications. One college reports taking written messages from classroom to classroom as an effective, reliable means to get crucial information to faculty and students.

- Don't forget the handy pocket telephone directory given to all. Be sure that your public information officer is prepared with critical media telephone numbers on his or her person.

- Be aware that even with the most thorough plan, primary individuals are likely to be unavailable. Have backup plans clearly stated.

INSTRUCTIONAL ISSUES

Only when a college emergency results in closure and missed class days will instructional issues become a significant part of the emergency recovery plan. Lost teaching days, loss of teaching spaces, and, as in the cases of Delgado Community College, Volunteer State Community College, and Pensacola Junior College, lost buildings and program areas all create havoc, with special trouble for programs such as nursing and allied health where students progress in groups toward specific certification tests and dates. Many faculty offices were lost with Katrina, Ivan, and the Tennessee tornadoes, and with them the books, notes, and records essential for faculty to teach.

Certain institutional practices can aid the college in its instructional recovery plan. When course outlines and syllabi are shared, electronic documents, the course can be recovered and reconfigured more easily and faculty can resume

information available to students on an ongoing basis: emergency hotlines and website access and addresses inform students of plans for reopening; training students in emergency preparedness through evacuation drills makes them safety conscious and ready to follow emergency instructions; and seeing their faculty take emergency preparedness seriously helps all. Included in course syllabi given to students each semester should be basic emergency information, including ways to contact the faculty member, department, or college if the college must close.

Colleges report that following emergency situations, their faculty recognized the need for building in course flexibility and providing online and other options for students. First-responder training programs became more popular, and all faculty recognized the value of such programs for students. Finally, faculty became more sensitive to the inclusion of environmental and safety issues within their courses.

When course objectives and outcomes are clearly defined, compressed scheduling and alternative delivery methods are more practical and applicable.

their work. When course objectives and outcomes are clearly defined, compressed scheduling and alternative delivery methods are more practical and applicable. When online courses provide options beyond the traditional classroom, students may resume their education as soon as electronic infrastructures can be repaired. Faculty at Pensacola Junior College were able to design a shortened term for teaching the clear course outcomes. More than 2,000 students were able to enroll in online course sections when Delgado was unable to open classrooms after the destruction of Katrina.

Besides advocating for course outline and syllabus clarity, colleges advise making emergency

PSYCHOLOGICAL ISSUES

Emotions become frayed when college students and employees live through disasters. In several situations, they suffered damage and destruction of their places of work and learning and of their homes. A Florida community college educator at Broward said, "The four successive hurricanes that hit our part of the state took a toll on students, faculty, and staff. Students were distracted from their studies; faculty were unable to cover the usual material; and lives were disrupted at work and at home. There was a loss of focus, direction, priorities, and [there was] huge stress throughout the college." Martha Ellis, president of Lee College, a college that was first used as an evacuation site for Hurricane Katrina and then had to evacuate a week later with the approach of Hurricane Rita, said, "There are long-

Community College in Gainesville, Florida, where an incident of domestic violence resulted in the death of an employee, provided opportunities for the college family to plant a tree and establish a

Be prepared to provide individual and group counseling, mediation services, grief and recovery workshops, and stress-management sessions for both students and employees.

term effects from such emergencies on people: physical, emotional, and spiritual."

Presidents say that colleges need to be prepared to provide individual and group counseling, mediation services, grief and recovery workshops, and stress-management sessions for both students and employees. Delgado made extensive use of agency referrals. Walter Bumphus, president of the Louisiana Community and Technical College System following Katrina, noted that there was a need for the colleges to go through the typical grieving process, with regressions happening as the crisis dragged on. Debriefings and emotional support sessions held by crisis counselors helped his employees and college leadership. Jackson Sasser at Santa Fe

memorial to the employee as a means of grieving. Often the provision of special recognition and a memorial service will occur on the anniversary of the tragic event.

As community colleges continue in our mission to educate those in our surrounding areas, it is not unexpected that societal and global issues will intrude onto our campuses. Preparation for terrorism, pandemics, weather emergencies, fires, and crime requires thoughtful planning and a willingness to imagine the worst. Through such efforts, we can be ready to face what the future holds with courage and intelligence.

Alice W. Villadsen is President Emeritus, Brookhaven College, Dallas County Community College District, Texas.

II.

Facing the Elements

Chapter 3

In Our Own Words: Disaster Recovery Post-Katrina

Walter G. Bumphus and Angel M. Royal

II.

Facing the Elements

Serving a population of 4.2 million people, the Louisiana Community and Technical College System's (LCTCS) institutions are located in 60 of the 64 parishes in the state. The LCTCS was created in 1999 as a means of providing an educational alternative to individuals who did not choose to pursue a four-year degree, but rather wanted to attain an associate degree, certificate, or diploma, which would ultimately lead them to the world of work. Like most traditional junior colleges, the LCTCS institutions previously had a strong emphasis on providing programs that transfer to two-year and four-year institutions. Now, in addition to that focus, the institutions have become more aggressive in responding to the state's workforce needs by providing relevant training programs, which are vital to economic development and assist in retaining current businesses and attracting new ones.

The Board of Supervisors of Community and Technical Colleges is a 17-member board, constitutionally required to be representative of the state's population by race and gender to ensure diversity. Fifteen of the members are appointed by the governor with consent of the Senate, and serve overlapping six-year terms. Two students serve on the board as well. The system is comprised of seven community colleges, two technical community colleges, and 40 technical college campuses organized into eight regions. Prior to the system's creation, several of the institutions that were being transitioned to the LCTCS were managed by the University of Louisiana System, and one institution,

which was created out of the desegregation settlement, was jointly managed by the Louisiana State University and Southern University Systems. The 40 technical campuses were previously managed by the Board of Elementary and Secondary Education. Another institution was created following the formal enactment of the system. This consolidation of two-year institutions into one system that could coordinate activities for the advancement of the state as a whole was difficult, yet necessary to ensure that Louisiana's citizens had market-driven, high-quality educational programs and services.

Collectively, the LCTCS institutions enroll about 60,000 students in credit and occupational training programs each semester. Prior to September 2005, the enrollment of the system's institutions had steadily increased. Three thousand full-time and 2,500 part-time faculty and staff are employed by the system and its institutions, and the organization has an annual operating budget in excess of $369 million. Many colleges and systems or districts across the country have the ability to tax locally; however, because of the extreme poverty in Louisiana, this funding stream does not exist. Operating budgets are generated through direct legislative appropriation, tuition and fees, and federal funding received by the institutions.

With robust enrollment and indications that additional funding would be infused into the two-year system by the Louisiana legislature to support growth and new initiatives, the picture for two-year education was promising.

ALONG CAME KATRINA: A DISASTER OF UNIMAGINABLE PROPORTIONS

Living along the Gulf Coast, one can never take too many precautions to prepare for the threat of hurricanes. For years the analogy of New Orleans as a fishbowl has been espoused, and scenarios of the city flooding after "the big one" makes its landfall have been the object of much speculation. Recollections of the devastation caused by Hurricane Betsy in 1965 and by Hurricane Andrew in 1992 have long been shared by survivors. Early on, when forecasters began projecting the strength and path of Hurricane Katrina, some chose to ignore the warnings because the state had escaped a serious brush with a catastrophic event for many years; others were unable to leave because of their socioeconomic status; and still others evacuated because they understood that Mother Nature is all powerful, and it is best to take precautions.

Four days prior to the hurricane's landfall, recognizing that cellular telephone service is faulty at best, the first act taken by the LCTCS was to campuses of the Louisiana Technical College are located in the Greater New Orleans Metropolitan Area. As the hurricane approached the Gulf of Mexico, the leadership of these institutions conferred and made a joint decision to close the institutions effective Saturday, August 27, through at least Tuesday, August 30. After the damage was assessed, the determination would be made regarding when to reopen the colleges. This decision was communicated by the colleges' leadership to the system president. Ultimately, Delgado and Nunez Community Colleges would have to make the determination to cancel the fall 2005 semester. Two campuses of the technical college remain closed today.

The State Office of Emergency Preparedness (OEP) convenes prior to any threat of natural disaster, specifically hurricanes, to track the storm's progress and strength, and to send immediate updates to major state agencies, their employees, and Louisiana's citizens. The system president is a member of the team assembled at OEP to receive briefings, and he, in turn

The first act taken by the LCTCS was to update its standard phone tree with pertinent contact information, including land lines, for board members, system staff responsible for critical operations, and the institutions' chief executive officers.

update its standard phone tree with pertinent contact information, including land lines, for board members, system staff responsible for critical operations, and the institutions' chief executive officers. This simple precautionary step would prove invaluable to the organization following the storm as cellular telephone service was inoperable in excess of two weeks. Delgado Community College, Nunez Community College, and four communicates to his leadership team and major personnel throughout the state. As news turned grimmer, the president issued stern words to the leadership of the institutions to "hunker down" if they were staying in New Orleans and the surrounding areas, and to travel safely if they were evacuating. The plan was to communicate after the storm passed to begin assessing damage and initiating the plan for the recovery.

Facing the Elements

Hurricane Katrina came ashore on August 29, 2005. Windspeeds over 140 miles per hour were recorded in southeast Louisiana, with gusts as high as 100 miles per hour in New Orleans. Rainfall exceeded 8 to 10 inches along the hurricane's path. Research compiled by the Louisiana Recovery Authority (LRA) places the total number of deaths from the storm at 1,464, with 135 people still missing. Twenty-two million tons of debris resulted from Katrina, which is enough to fill the Empire State Building forty times.

In higher education, about 84,000 students were displaced, which includes 39.6 percent of the enrollment of the LCTCS; 1,400 system employees were also displaced. Delgado Community College's City Park campus in mid-city New Orleans experienced damage to 20 of its 25 buildings. Every building on Nunez Community College was inundated with flood waters of over six feet, which necessitated gutting all the first floors. Two campuses of the Louisiana Technical College, Sidney Collier and Slidell, were also affected, with the Sidney Collier campus being completely destroyed. Collier is located in the lower Ninth Ward. Damage estimates exceed $100 million.

MAJOR EFFECTS OF KATRINA ON LCTCS

- 84,000 higher education students displaced
- 1,400 LCTCS employees displaced
- 20 of 25 buildings damaged at Delgado Community College City Park campus
- More than six feet of flood water in every building at Nunez Community College
- Complete destruction of Louisiana Technical College's Sidney Collier campus

---

The LCTCS office is located in Baton Rouge, Louisiana. While the entire southeast region of the state felt the impact of Hurricane Katrina, the effect on Baton Rouge, approximately 80 miles from New Orleans, was minimal when compared with what happened in that region. While the system office itself retained power, there were widespread traffic light and power outages throughout the Baton Rouge area, which lasted for about four days following the storm. In addition, gasoline availability was nonexistent in excess of a week, making travel extremely difficult.

Like the rest of the nation, the system watched in disbelief the events that unfolded in the Greater New Orleans Metropolitan Area over the days and weeks following Katrina. Although the LCTCS was aware of potential issues prior to the storms and had a disaster recovery plan in place, like the State of Louisiana, the organization could not anticipate the widespread devastation or the amount of time that would pass before people could even re-enter the region. Like the individuals who evacuated the city anticipating returning home within about four days, the system leadership was shocked to learn that it would be months before people could safely re-enter the region because of environmental concerns. The current disaster recovery plan was clearly not going to address this devastating situation.

Once the initial shock over the magnitude of the storm passed, communication began. The system president immediately made contact with each chief executive officer of the colleges to determine whether they were safe and to ascertain their location. Two had evacuated to Houston and one to North Carolina. The CEO who could not be reached had chosen to stay in St. Bernard Parish, one of the hardest hit regions on the Gulf Coast. It would be days before the system received notification that he had survived and was safe. The chief executive officers and president agreed to meet the week following the storm, but would remain in frequent contact via telephone.

At the same time, all the system presidents and college chancellors and presidents in higher education were convened by the Louisiana Board of Regents to share information and discuss the coordination of services to assist with the recovery of the region and the affected students, faculty, and staff.

OUR IMMEDIATE ACTIONS: DISASTER RESPONSE FOR THE RECOVERY OF OUR STUDENTS AND OUR INSTITUTIONS

While the LCTCS and each institution have disaster recovery plans, the magnitude of this catastrophe called for a dramatic departure from those plans and the writing of a new one as response to the storm unfolded. In addition to dealing with the routine facility damage issues, students enrolled in the last semester of their programs had been displaced and needed assistance to achieve their educational goals. Also, students, faculty, and staff were displaced across the country. Specifically, the system staff had to deal with communications, operations, student services, and employment challenges. To do this, the system president assembled his core

and vice president of external affairs communicated to the higher education community, elected officials, and the two-year colleges and organizations across the country.

The first step was the establishment of a call center to identify displaced employees and students, to gather contact information, and to answer their questions. This number was posted on the website, provided on voice recordings on all office phones, and communicated through the Louisiana Board of Regents. Next, a website was launched to provide status reports and the most up-to-date information to employees and students affected by the hurricanes. Those outside of the state would be able to access the internet. Public service announcements were developed and distributed statewide to inform students and employees about contacting their colleges. Ads were

Meetings for faculty, staff, and students of the affected institutions were hosted to provide information and answer questions.

administrative team, which includes the senior vice presidents for finance and administration, academic and student affairs, and workforce and economic development, the executive assistant to the president and vice president for external affairs, the director of public information, and the director of internal audit. He immediately appointed the director of internal audit to serve as the point of contact and to coordinate all Federal Emergency Management Agency (FEMA) issues.

Communications. Even in ideal situations, communication is always cited as a challenge. This challenge was compounded by the fact that power outages prevented many people from accessing the internet and cellular phone service was nonexistent. The director of public information served as the point of contact on all media communication for the system, and the executive assistant to the president

also placed in *Dallas Morning News, Houston Chronicle, Atlanta Constitution Journal, Times Picayune* (New Orleans), *The Advocate* (Baton Rouge), and *The News Star* (Monroe) to communicate with displaced staff and students.

Outside of the critical external communications, the system established hurricane updates to inform legislators, stakeholders, and national organizations about what was occurring during the aftermath of the storm and throughout the recovery. As this disaster unfolded, there was overwhelming support from organizations and colleges across the country offering financial assistance. The system immediately established guidelines for an LCTCS Hurricane Katrina Relief Fund. Phone calls were made to the United States Department of Education and the Southern Association of Colleges and

Schools Commission on Colleges to provide them with a status report on the affected institutions. Weekly meetings with the chancellors of the affected institutions were also scheduled, and one of the most important actions was to have phone meetings with the Florida Community College System leadership to discuss the recovery, as

payroll processing system. The system office was already centrally processing the payroll for Nunez Community College and the campuses of the technical college, so this process continued following the storm. For Delgado, the situation was more difficult because the institution was not on the centralized system. On a positive note, backup

Make sure the institution's disaster recovery plan includes a backup site for pertinent records in another state.

Florida had also experienced a series of major disasters a few years earlier.

Although faculty and staff were dispersed across the country, many remained in the Greater Baton Rouge Metropolitan Area and the region, so meetings for faculty, staff, and students of the affected institutions were hosted to provide information and answer questions.

Operations. Immediately following the hurricane, damage to the institutions could not be assessed, so it was important to establish a base of operations. This base needed to be centrally located to serve faculty, staff, and students. The system president worked with the chancellor of Baton Rouge Community College to identify administrative office space that could be reconfigured to house the major administrative staffs of Delgado and Nunez Community Colleges. Because the Louisiana Technical College's central administration was also housed in Baton Rouge, the affected technical college campuses established a temporary location with the central office. The system's information technology staff immediately began the process of setting up computers and telephone lines for the temporary offices, establishing Blackberry services for key personnel, and working with the institutions to re-establish information technology connectivity.

Of immediate importance was the need to process payroll for the displaced employees. Of the LCTCS institutions, three are not on a centralized

records for that institution were housed off site. Unfortunately, news is that those backup records were located in the New Orleans area, which was not accessible. This was a valuable lesson learned: Make sure the institution's disaster recovery plan includes a backup site for pertinent records in another state. As a result of this challenge, system staff assisted with data entry for more than 900 Delgado employees in order for them to receive payroll checks. The system staff also facilitated the transfer of funds from Delgado to the LCTCS for payroll related to Delgado employees. After the checks were processed, the most efficient means of delivering them had to be determined. Many banks were closed, and because the payroll had been recreated, direct deposit of the funds was not an option. If employees contacted the call center, provided a temporary address, and verified pertinent information, the check was mailed. If they came in person to the office, they had to provide identification, and the check was released. Paying people during this devastating time was one of the system's proudest accomplishments.

Student Services. Of all the challenges that had to be addressed, it was paramount to attend to the students whose lives had been completely disrupted. There were financial aid considerations to address in addition to tuition issues and academic matters. First, the Louisiana Board of Regents and the Louisiana Office of Student Financial Assistance (LOSFA) worked with the U.S. Department of Education to establish parameters for addressing financial aid disbursements that occurred prior to Hurricane Katrina, and to address the matter of students re-enrolling at other institutions and accessing any remaining funds. Second, the Board of Regents urged, and all of higher education agreed, to allow students to re-enroll in other two-year or four-year institutions during the fall 2005 semester without regard for the payment of additional tuition or the presentation of transcripts, as most records were not accessible to students or staff. Supplying records and tuition issues were to be addressed in the spring of 2006.

Providing continuity to assist students with achieving their academic goals was a very difficult issue to address because each student issue is unique. For example, many nursing students in the final semester of their program were displaced across the country. To meet these students' needs, the system academic staff worked with the institutional leadership and the institutions across the country where students were displaced. The American Association of Community Colleges (AACC) was a major partner assisting in this effort. The association served as the clearinghouse for the many offers of support from two-year institutions across the country. The Sloan Semester offered by the Southern Regional Education Board was also invaluable, as it allowed students to enroll in online courses free of charge. The Lumina Foundation for Education and Scholarship America also provided integral services by establishing a relief fund enabling students who re-enrolled in another institution to access assistance through the financial aid office at the institution where they were relocating. In addition, counseling was provided by some LCTCS institutions to assist the many grieving students and employees in coming to terms with this life-changing event.

Employment. Prior to the realization of major budget challenges, public postsecondary education institutions agreed to continue paying displaced faculty and staff until a determination could be made about the fiscal outlook for the state. Further, if displaced employees relocated to other areas of the state, they could provide teaching or administrative services to a higher education institution located within the region, but would not

get paid twice for providing those services. This employment arrangement was to be reported to the home institution. Many displaced individuals continued to receive salary and benefits until November 2005.

By October 2005, with the bleak budget picture, the decision had to be made for institutions to reduce their workforce between 20 and 40 percent, through force majeure policies instituted by all higher education systems following the storms. Each college chancellor was responsible for working with the system staff to develop a plan to furlough and lay off employees the institution could no longer sustain. The system president presented these plans to the board of supervisors for approval. This decision was truly agonizing for all chief executive officers because it meant terminating the employment of many people who had lost all their worldly possessions and were struggling with a host of other emotional and personal issues.

However, with all that the system, its institutions, employees, and students have gone through, the LCTCS continues "Changing Lives, and Creating Futures" on the long road of recovery.

OUR LESSONS LEARNED

As a result of Hurricane Katrina, the system was prepared for another devastating blow, Hurricane Rita, which made landfall in southwest Louisiana on September 24, 2005. In addition, the recovery activities greatly assisted the system and its institutions in crafting more relevant disaster recovery plans. Now, routine meetings are conducted to ensure that disaster preparation is at the forefront of thought always.

Safety and security are two of the most important considerations when dealing with a natural disaster. It is always better to err on the side of caution. Based on experiences with Hurricanes Katrina and Rita, the Louisiana Community and Technical College System designed a checklist to assist its colleges with disaster preparations. This checklist may prove helpful to other institutions as it can be modified to other disaster situations.

LCTCS Disaster Preparedness Checklist

☐ 1. Send a communication to college employees notifying them of the potential threat.

  ☐ a. Give them helpful advice on securing their property and making preparations.

  ☐ b. Tell them how to contact the college in the event that the disaster impacts the normal operations.

☐ 2. For safety, make the decision well in advance if college closure is appropriate.

☐ 3. Establish a phone tree which includes cell phone and land-line numbers for all essential employees. All numbers should be provided since cell phones are not always reliable.

☐ 4. Back up all student, human resource, and financial records. Also develop a process for pending human resource issues (e.g., new hires and hourly employees).

☐ 5. Pack essential equipment, including laptops, and take them in the event that a temporary location has to be established.

☐ 6. Check the institution's property listing for accuracy today. Update immediately if necessary.

☐ 7. Take a digital camera and get pictures of all of the college facilities before the disaster.

☐ 8. Be prepared to set up an alternative site for college operations where essential staff can meet and focus on next steps.

☐ 9. Secure all college and campus facilities. In the case of severe weather, ensure that all objects on the college perimeter that can become projectile objects with high winds have been brought into the facility. If a business located near the college or campus has loose objects near it, talk to the business about securing those items. Prepare to cover any windows with plywood, if applicable.

☐ 10. Designate a FEMA point person for your institution, so that if your college receives any damage, you can register immediately and have a centralized person coordinating these efforts for you.

☐ 11. Immediately following exposure, contact the system president to discuss the status of the college or campus and its operations.

☐ 12. In the event the college closes for an extended period of time, develop a plan to track and monitor employees and students.

☐ 13. Appoint one point of contact to communicate with the media on behalf of the college.

☐ 14. Identify the point person who has all keys and codes to enter the facility. Make sure that person is available to assess the state of the facilities.

☐ 15. Purchase satellite telephones for key personnel to use in the event that phone service is disrupted.

☐ 16. The institution should already have a backup facility for records in another state that is not prone to experience the same type of natural disaster.

Walter G. Bumphus is President Emeritus, Louisiana Community and Technical College System, and Angel M. Royal is Executive Assistant to the President and Vice President for External Affairs, Louisiana Community and Technical College System.

Chapter 4

The Katrina Disaster: Delgado Community College Response and Recovery

Alice W. Villadsen and Alex Johnson

Facing the Elements

Prior to the devastation of Hurricane Katrina at the beginning of the fall 2005 semester, Delgado Community College in New Orleans was a college on the move. The largest of the Louisiana Community and Technical College System members, Delgado enrolled 17,400 credit students on eight campuses and centers throughout the New Orleans area. Under the leadership of Chancellor Alex Johnson, Delgado had refocused its energy and vision on being a learning college with major emphasis on meeting the economic development needs of its full service area, including some of the most economically depressed metropolitan areas. Workforce Training Solutions had been recently implemented as a mechanism to bring job-related skills training to the underskilled local population. Nationally ranked programs in the health sciences complemented the college's comprehensive mission. New facilities and renovations had been completed, and the college's pride was evident. "Excellence through Opportunity" was the motto that gave voice to Delgado's ambitious goal of increasing income through resource development initiatives. Delgado had also launched a new marketing and public relations effort resulting in significant enrollment growth.

Although New Orleans includes many locations that are situated below sea or river level and it is surrounded by the Gulf of Mexico, Lake Pontchartrain, and the Mississippi River, a series of levees had for scores of years kept the city relatively free of major flooding. And hurricanes had been infrequent, sometimes skirting the New Orleans

area but never scoring a direct hit. Delgado had formulated a hurricane disaster plan as a part of its general emergency plans but had not been required to test the plan since New Orleans had been so fortunate in averting such disasters.

DISASTER STRIKES

Although Katrina, a Category 5 hurricane, was a fearful storm, its lengthy approach through the Gulf of Mexico in late August 2005, after it had hit southern Florida as a Category 1 hurricane, was erratic. Targets for possible landfall included the city of New Orleans, and the city was in the process of evacuating when finally, about 24 hours before predicted landfall, the storm veered toward the Mississippi/Alabama coastline and away from New Orleans. With gridlock on the exit routes from the city, air service cancelled, and a large population of residents stranded, local authorities were beginning to feel relief that the city was to be spared again. Sure enough, the winds of the monster storm tracked east, and the huge storm surge hit the Mississippi coast at landfall.

The storm itself did little damage to New Orleans and its immediate metropolitan areas. But just as the collective sigh of relief was being made, the unseen devastation of the giant storm became apparent in the city: The levees failed. Within minutes, the waters surrounding the city, specifically the waters of Lake Pontchartrain, began pouring into New Orleans neighborhoods. The traditionally vulnerable spots were immediately flooded and, as the waters continued to rise, areas of the city that had never been flooded were also soon underwater. The primary issue of those left in the city was simple survival, somehow getting higher than the water. The horror of the next week has been documented, indeed, emblazoned on our college minds' eyes: house-top rescues; evacuees swarming to the Superdome; families bereft of shelter, food, clothing, health care; and more than 1,000 deaths.

Delgado shared in the community disaster. Photographs show a college under water, classrooms and buildings either destroyed or horribly damaged, roadways leading to the college sites inaccessible. Delgado Chancellor Alex Johnson and his family had evacuated to Atlanta; students

heads of information technology, communications, finance, payroll, human resources, and compliance; the website coordinator; and the directors of facilities, financial aid, and public safety. He also added a curriculum expert, a proposal writer, and, very importantly, a person charged with government and agency relations.

The first task was to locate a temporary administrative space for the team headquarters since the college's administrative building was uninhabitable and inaccessible. Many crucial staff had no homes or found their homes inaccessible, so temporary housing and office space were found for them. Johnson marveled at the dedication and professionalism of these team members who had to set aside their personal losses and concentrate with him on the college crisis. However, all

The scope of the devastation obliterated any preconceived emergency plan.

and staff were displaced or in missions; many fled to places throughout the Southeastern United States and Texas. There was loss of life, property, stability, and work for students and staff. The college's highly successful fall semester was simply cancelled. The scope of the devastation obliterated any preconceived emergency plan.

RESPONDING TO THE DISASTER

The president, upon his immediate return to the New Orleans area, was able to communicate with a remnant of his college leadership who were also returning. Once minimal communications were established, Johnson knew that his first step had to be the creation of a new Emergency Response Team (ERT) made up of individuals who were essential in handling the immediate crisis. His first ERT included, along with himself, the

immediately endorsed the logical goal for the team: the college would reopen as soon as humanly possible. This goal – reopening Delgado – became the focus of the team's work over the next crucial weeks and months.

During the earliest days following Katrina, the role of the chancellor was to set direction and tone for the recovery. He had to be decisive and make quick decisions, sometimes alone. He found that he had to be demanding in the crisis yet conscientious and reassuring, constantly available to all, and resilient personally. He quickly became the face of the institution to local media. His role as the advocate for the college's survival and recovery became crucial. And he had to take responsibility, much beyond any time previously, to be the institution's memory.

Based upon the early decision to reopen Delgado as soon as possible and serve the needs of its students, particularly students in health programs whose progress toward certification was essential, these first steps were taken:

- Determine the status of facilities and locate temporary quarters.

- Restore information technology functions, including the website, online course capacity, and student administrative systems.

- Launch a public relations campaign so that everyone received regular status reports.

- Secure approval to implement administrative processes that expedited reopening the college and providing education options for students.

- Locate students and, where possible, retain them in online courses, provide them with direct instruction at a remote location, or transfer them to other colleges nearby.

Delgado proudly reopened all sites by the second semester, January 2006, with 10,008 students re-enrolling. Of those students, 25 percent enrolled online. Fifty-five percent of "Pre-K" employees at the college remained and were working that January. The college took the opportunity to continue to expand its education and training role in the community, and strong linkages were made with the Louisiana technical colleges. With the support of the Southern Association of Colleges and Schools, Delgado refined its quality focus in the reaccreditation process. Strong new, renewed, and traditional involvements with governmental agencies resulted from the college tragedy. Community colleges from Southern states and Texas came to the rescue of Delgado's students by

institutional and state regulations to benefit and provide a temporary educational home for students.

Since Katrina and the reopening of Delgado Community College, the college has continued to recover the infrastructure that was destroyed or damaged by the hurricane and has worked hard to stabilize the financial health of the institution. Because of the need to use online instruction and other alternative means of providing distance instruction in response to student displacement and needs, Delgado has revamped its organizational structure and instructional delivery. It has been important for Delgado to ensure that there is a critical mass of faculty and staff to do the work of the college. It has become an even stronger leader in workforce development initiatives in the region. Of course, the renovation and rebuilding of college facilities has been crucial as Delgado has remained actively involved with its college stakeholders, organizations, and agencies.

REVIEW, EVALUATION, AND LESSONS LEARNED

A storm of the century like Katrina overcomes almost any college emergency plan with the scope of its devastation. However, looking back on the lessons of August 2005, Johnson sees certain actions as crucial for colleges preparing for the worst:

Identify an emergency response team early, certainly prior to any emergency. But realize that the emergency itself may make that team unavailable, so backup membership is crucial as well. Provide the emergency response team with

The college took the opportunity to continue to expand its education and training role in the community.

accepting them as transfer students well into the fall semester, often at free or significantly reduced tuition and often with emergency changes in

laptop computers and cell phones with alternative area codes. The New Orleans area codes were not workable because of damage to the cell towers in the area. Have a logical alternative location identified assuming that the college cannot be used by the emergency team. Ensure that the team has housing and take responsibility for finding such alternative housing.

Secure information technology. If your system is located in basement or first floor areas in flood prone communities, relocate this critical operation to higher floors. Document retrieval for student records, payroll, and other significant administrative functions is imperative, so portable systems and backup systems become crucial. Often, a distant hotsite is important, with some community colleges finding partner colleges in other parts of the country. Secure storage for instructional materials, especially course syllabi and outlines, can be hugely important when classes have to be relocated or alternate faculty become involved in teaching.

Implement a communications plan. Electronic means for communication following the first few days or weeks of a major emergency become essential. Delgado used its website to communicate with students and employees, and chat rooms proved helpful in sharing information and answering questions. Strong partnerships with local and national media proved invaluable as information needed to be provided about student and employee safety, college decisions, and plans for reopening not only in the New Orleans area but also throughout the country since so many had evacuated beyond the normal service area. The president and public information officer provided periodic updates and press releases on policies, facilities, programs, and people. The president also found it important to have strong

advice from his editorial board and public information professionals about language and appropriate statements to the press.

Cultivate relationships with federal, state, and local agencies. With Katrina, the crucial agencies with which Delgado kept constant contact were the state's higher education coordinating agency (LaHERT); key legislators and executives at the state and federal levels (Department of Education, Labor, and Congressional Black Caucus); professional organizations, including the American Association of Community Colleges, American Council on Education, the League for Innovation in the Community College, and, of course, regional accrediting bodies. Advisory groups also can prove helpful during crisis times: college program advisory councils, and local governmental agencies and councils.

Provide group and individual counseling services for both employees and students. Helping to alleviate a variety of difficult personal and interpersonal challenges became a crucial service for the college to provide either through direct counseling or through referrals. Important to Delgado were the efforts of "Global Nomads" and programs such as "Coping with Grief and Loss" (Case Western Reserve University) and APA's "Managing Stress: After the Hurricanes." Managing stress through mediation instruction proved important to those affected. And through it all, Delgado attempted to realize its responsibility to treat the whole person even though a major part of services were to aid students in continuing their educational progress as quickly as possible.

> ## CRUCIAL FACTORS IN EMERGENCY RESPONSE
>
> 1. Identify an emergency response team, including backup membership, prior to any emergency.
> 2. Secure information technology.
> 3. Implement a communications plan.
> 4. Cultivate relationships with federal, state, and local agencies.
> 5. Provide group and individual counseling services for employees and students.
> 6. Establish an emergency preparedness checklist to supplement the emergency plan.

Establish an emergency preparedness checklist to supplement the college's emergency plan. This checklist should include three components: preparations for a state of emergency; operations in a state of emergency; and immediate recovery from a state of emergency. Johnson believes that in all

Before Hurricane Katrina, Delgado Community College had made significant strides as a learning-centered institution. This progress must now serve as the framework for a major shift in the learning-college approach, one that must facilitate learning and, simultaneously,

Helping to alleviate a variety of difficult personal and interpersonal challenges became a crucial service for the college to provide either through direct counseling or through referrals.

cases, it is highly important to get the college facilities open as quickly as possible and sees that imperative as an important focus for the college administration, faculty, staff, and students, a rallying cry to action.

Normalcy at Delgado and normalcy for New Orleans may be truly years away because of the continuing impact on facilities and funding that Hurricane Katrina left in its wake. However, a return to operations as quickly as possible worked as an operational guideline for Delgado. Johnson stated, just six months following Katrina:

challenge us to experiment with new approaches to producing learners. There are no roadmaps for this effort, no benchmarks for a learning college affected by a natural disaster. But what we do possess is collective wisdom, creativity, and experience. And it is these attributes that will serve us steadfastly as we produce learners for a new economy.

Alice W. Villadsen is President Emeritus, Brookhaven College, Dallas County Community College District, Texas, and Alex Johnson is Chancellor, Delgado Community

Chapter 5

The Rigors of Paradise:
Miami Dade College Responds to Hurricane Katrina

Theodore Levitt

Facing the Elements

Miami Dade College (MDC) is located in Miami-Dade County, Florida. Eight campuses and several outreach centers spread across the 2,000 square miles of the county, serving the area's more than 2.3 million residents. MDC is among the largest higher education institutions in the United States, enrolling more than 160,000 students in a full range of Associate in Science, Associate in Arts, Bachelor of Science (Education and Public Safety Management), and professional certification programs. The college is governed by a seven-member district board of trustees and a college president, and is one of 28 institutions that comprise Florida's community college system.

PLANNING FOR DISASTER

Miami Dade College is guided in its preparation and response to disaster by a comprehensive emergency management plan. The plan addresses all aspects of communication and safety awareness for students and employees, as well as thorough preparation and response protocols for all aspects of college functioning, in particular the preservation of the physical plant, business operations, and information technology resources.

The process of preparation and response to each disaster event is led by the college's emergency management team (EMT), composed of the college president, campus presidents, provosts, members of the college president's senior staff, including the director of communications, and relevant vice provosts. This group convenes at least once per day

before, during, and after a storm. They do so in person or via conference call, and are equipped with pocket directories with contact information for all members of the EMT as well as college and campus executive leadership. When the storm has passed, the EMT also sets priorities for recovery efforts and maintains communication with all sectors of the college and larger community.

The facilities operations plan details the functioning of the operations center; key personnel, also identifying essential personnel within the areas of facilities and plant maintenance; and general preparedness that includes activities prior to hurricane season and progressive steps to be executed during hurricane watch, hurricane warning, and post-storm. The plan also identifies particular document preparation for insurance and FEMA claims as well as different types of expenditures in the aftermath of a storm.

The college's Department of Communications also follows a standard protocol with the approach of a storm. The tools include informational releases to media outlets and governmental agencies; website postings; two telephone hotlines, one general and one with specific direction for essential employees in security and maintenance; collegewide email messages from the college president to all employees and students at least once per day, as well as voice messages to all employees.

MDC's Business Affairs Department also implements a contingency plan to ensure smooth functioning of all essential district administrative functions. Backup plans provide avenues to maintain all departmental functioning with regard to payroll, finances, accounting, purchasing and risk management.

Information technology focuses on protecting the integrity of critical business functions, with the aim of resuming these services within 24 hours following a disaster. Secondary business functions aim to recommence within five business days following a disaster. Achieving these deadlines is accomplished by providing a group of department core teams that will be available to any

before turning it sharply south-southwest through Miami-Dade County. Katrina made landfall around 6:30 p.m., Thursday, August 25, near the Broward/Miami-Dade County border. The storm registered as Category 1 on the Safir-Simpson scale, though maximum winds were clocked at 97 mph as it sliced across central and southwest Miami-Dade County. The storm dumped heavy rains, measuring between 12 and 16 inches at various sites in the county. Ironically, the storm appeared spent when it exited the Florida peninsula, tamed somewhat by

Information technology focuses on protecting the integrity of critical business functions.

department(s) affected by a disaster. The core teams, in addition to directing the recovery efforts, ensure that the resources required by the departments are made available as quickly as possible.

DISASTER STRIKES: KATRINA COMES TO MIAMI

Before Hurricane Katrina whipped through Louisiana and Mississippi, it wreaked what appeared to be minor havoc in South Florida. All is, indeed, relative in hurricane country, as the storm spurred a full disaster response from Miami Dade College and in the end caused significant damage to the physical plant.

MDC personnel monitor every storm from inception, maintaining close communication with Miami-Dade County's Office of Emergency Management. Katrina emerged as a tropical wave off the west coast of Africa and grew into a tropical depression about 175 miles southeast of Nassau in the Bahamas on August 23, 2005. The following day she became a tropical storm and moved northwestward through the Bahamas.

Our hope was that the storm would continue on that path, sparing South Florida and with a little luck, tracking out to sea. But the conspiring winds bent the storm west and south toward South Florida

the landmass. But true to form, over the warm open waters of the gulf, Katrina would achieve Category 5 status by August 28 as it veered north to the Bayou.

Each year, MDC's Emergency Management Team and essential personnel within the Facilities Management area, conduct planning meetings on May 1, one month before the official start of the hurricane season (June 1 – November 30). Hurricane procedures are reviewed and information and supplies updated. To be sure, this is a plan that has been put to the test and adjusted many times, and is now well positioned to respond to major storms.

The Facilities Emergency Management Plan for hurricanes is divided into several sections that include preseason preparation and the warning stages of an approaching storm. Hurricane watch, indicating approaching hurricane conditions within 36 hours, hurricane warning, indicating approaching hurricane conditions within 24 hours, and post-storm sections call for specific protective, evaluation, and restoration procedures.

The preseason preparation is divided by departments, including Facilities Design and Construction, Plant Maintenance, and the Facilities Planning Department. Checklists for each department detail necessary steps in preparing for storm season. The most significant steps are listed on page 38.

Facing the Elements

PARTIAL CHECKLIST, FACILITIES DESIGN AND CONSTRUCTION DEPARTMENT

❑ Damage assessment kits prepared

❑ Phone and address lists/phone tree updated

❑ Emergency contractor list updated

❑ Necessary equipment and supplies in ready order

❑ Update list of hazards, storage, documentation, and safety protocols

❑ Conduct in-house seminar with assessment team; review methodology

❑ Review team responsibilities and backups at every level

❑ Review hazardous conditions in specific buildings

PARTIAL CHECKLIST, PLANT MAINTENANCE DEPARTMENT

❑ Fill sandbags and distribute to all campus and center holding areas

❑ Ensure all shutters in working order

❑ Ensure secure locations for plywood and 2x4 lumber

❑ Check all traffic signs for loose bolts

❑ Check operation of generators, saws, and other equipment for emergency use

❑ Review staff availability and assignments during storm

❑ Refill emergency drinking water supply

Command centers are established at each of MDC's eight campuses. Each is equipped with primary and backup phone lines. At least two employees from security or facilities remain in a safe location on campus to maintain contact with decision makers and provide immediate assessments of damage.

Information technology (IT) implements a series of procedures to protect records and equipment. Potential hurricane conditions require a number of backup operations, including mainframe and network. In addition, the feasibility of running an early payroll is always explored, given that such an operation requires six hours. IT also makes immediate contact with the college's storage provider, Iron Mountain (FORTRESS), to arrange for pick-up and return delivery of critical records.

The College President's Office and the Department of Communications work together to prepare the entire college community for the approach of hurricane season. A preseason message from the president is issued via email and the college website to both students and employees. MDC has more than 125,000 email addresses for students and nearly 100 percent coverage for employees. The message emphasizes personal responsibility to secure work and home; provides a checklist for supplies and preparation for home and family; lists communication vehicles, including hotline phone numbers, website addresses, and local media; and offers instructions on how to communicate the need for personal or family support following the storm.

As Katrina approached, the college's Department of Communications began to exercise standard protocols. A bulletin on the homepage of the MDC website, accompanied by a forecast track, announced the need to prepare in advance to shut down operations in the event that the storm continued to threaten South Florida. Similar messages were loaded into the hotlines. The department also issued a press release, advising the media of the institution's preparations for the storm. The instant a hurricane watch was declared and updated email messages were sent from the president, alerts were placed on the website, hotlines, and voicemail messages.

With the announcement of a hurricane warning, indicating hurricane conditions in the next 24 hours, a second set of protocols went into effect. The Emergency Planning Team immediately convened via conference call and issued a message through all communication vehicles announcing the closing of Miami Dade College as of noon on Wednesday,

County. Category 1 storms like Katrina are tolerated as part of the price of paradise. But experience has shown the residents of this region that inconvenience, destruction, and even tragedy are threatened in the most modest of storms. The wind damage from Hurricane Wilma, a Category 2 storm that struck three months after Katrina, left South Floridians without water and power for weeks. Thousands of roofs were left in disrepair over the ensuing year.

Media releases continued while the college was closed, providing an additional source of information for students, employees, and the public.

August 24. The message urged everyone to stay in regular contact with the hotlines or website for daily status updates. A media release was also issued.

All facilities departments began to lock down the physical plant and equipment in the run-up to the storm. Checks on damage assessment kits, preparation of advance emergency purchase orders, shutdown of gas lines to science labs, removal of nonessential antennas, securing all equipment, and tamping down to emergency electricity levels in parking lots and campus streets reflect the numerous lock down and final procedures to ready for Katrina.

Across MDC's eight campuses, employees engaged in a familiar ritual as computers were unplugged and reams of plastic unfolded across desks and equipment. Then, they made their way into the eerily pleasant day-before-the-storm weather and final preparations on the home front.

RESPONDING TO THE DISASTER

All storms in South Florida are measured against Hurricane Andrew, the 1992 tempest that overwhelmed the southern half of Miami-Dade

Katrina also inflicted severe damage, most of it the result of flooding from the heavy rains. The college remained closed until the following Monday, August 29. The preparation procedures were executed effectively and administrative and facilities personnel continued to communicate throughout the storm and its aftermath. Daily communications, from the time the college closed on Wednesday, August 24, until reopening on August 29, occurred with the Emergency Management Team and the campus facility liaisons. The college hotlines and website provided daily updates to students and college personnel. Media releases continued while the college was closed, providing an additional source of information for students, employees, and the public.

Katrina brought no serious harm to students or employees of MDC. However, damages were extensive at the campuses and immediate post-storm protocols were implemented. Prior to two-person assessment teams touring all the buildings at each campus, representatives of the construction department verified that no hazardous conditions or materials posed imminent danger. Construction personnel also evaluated the safety of electrical, gas, and fuel systems, and ensured that disconnects were performed where required. Safe ventilation was also verified. Wherever required, signage indicating "Unsafe Structure/No Trespassing" was posted.

The two-person assessment teams identified the scope by recording detailed descriptions, photographing the conditions, and attempting to quantify the damage. They also recorded expert analysis from electrical and air conditioning inspectors. Based on initial assessments, plant maintenance personnel made basic emergency repairs wherever possible to prevent further damage. Campus planning staff began to coordinate with campus teams to implement clean up of debris.

Initial reports from the campuses indicated varying degrees of water intrusion at all campuses. The Kendall Campus and Homestead Campus, both in the southern end of the county, reported a total 125 rooms with water damage. Downed trees and vegetative damage were the other major damage elements, with some minor roof damage. On Friday, following the initial assessment effort, the vice provost for facilities projected the strong likelihood of reopening the college on Monday. College work crews and contractors were on site and working around the clock to clear debris and

Campus. Reports from Florida Power and Light regarding restoration of power ranged from Sunday morning to Sunday evening. Homestead was officially projected for a Tuesday morning opening. Additional equipment was called in for Sunday morning to address the parking lots and classroom standing water. Blowers would be needed all week to protect against mold accumulation. The Entrepreneurial Education Center, however, delivered good news: Power was back and MEEC would open on Monday.

Recovery efforts. For the purpose of disaster assessment, MDC's eight campuses and several outreach centers are divided into three zones. Zone 1 includes North and Hialeah campuses, the Meek Entrepreneurial Center, and Miami International Airport Center; Zone 2 encompasses Kendall, Homestead, and West Campuses and the Tamiami Airport Center; and Zone 3 consists of Wolfson, Medical, and InterAmerican Campuses and the New World School of the Arts, a high school/college partnership program proximate to the Wolfson Campus in downtown Miami.

North and Kendall Campuses are MDC's oldest and largest locations, with 19 buildings at North and 14 buildings at Kendall. Both are sprawling

Our approach has been to explore every possible avenue to maximize safety and protect the operations of the college.

pump out standing water. Questionable for Monday opening were the Carrie Meek Entrepreneurial Education Center (MEEC) and the Homestead Campus. MEEC had no power or functioning backup generator as of Friday, meaning the air conditioning was off line. Homestead had more than two feet of standing water in the parking areas and many classrooms in need of water removal.

A Saturday update indicated that most facilities across the college's campuses were fully operational. Major concerns as of 6:00 p.m. included six buildings without power at the Kendall

campuses with lush tropical environs. The remaining campuses are more urban, with the Wolfson Campus and its seven buildings situated in the heart of downtown Miami. Homestead, InterAmerican, Medical, Hialeah, and West campuses and the centers are decidedly smaller.

Total damage in the three zones was established at more than $1.77 million. Zone 2, located in the southern sector of Miami-Dade County, was hardest hit by Katrina. Damages for the zone totaled more than $1.1 million, with just over $630,000 assigned to remedy water intrusion. The remainder of the damage estimate covered uprooted trees and other vegetation. Similar damage was found in the other zones, with Zone 1 in the northern end of the county totaling $533,200 in repair needs and Zone 3 in the more urban, downtown areas of the city showing damages at $124,750.

The college's primary aim following a storm is to restore safety for students and employees and reopen for classes and operations as quickly as possible. Using customary vendors, MDC addresses emergency repairs that will accomplish the required safety levels to allow for reopening.

MDC is insured through a consortium or a risk-sharing pool with 26 other community colleges throughout Florida. This approach covers the initial $2.5 million dollars of damages for the entire consortium for a given storm. Beyond $2.5 million, an excess carrier comes into play for the next $10 million. To date, this second level of coverage has been adequate to cover damages for the consortium.

Following Katrina, MDC's risk management department contacted the consortium to report serious damages. In turn, the consortium notified its third party administrator/adjuster, Gallagher Bassett, which dispatched its on-site adjuster to survey the damages and provide a general notation of such to the Gallagher Bassett office. MDC's facilities representatives and contractors also surveyed the scope of damages and estimates were sent to Gallagher Bassett. Once the work was completed, invoices were forwarded to Gallagher Bassett and payment was released to the college and to contractors.

While the college lost just three days of classes and operations to Katrina, damage repair continued for another two to four weeks at various campuses to replace trees and vegetation and ensure that water damage had no lasting effects.

LEARNING FROM DISASTER

The primary and continuing lesson for hurricane and disaster preparedness is thorough preparation. This can be a time-consuming

endeavor for a large institution like MDC, but all the more critical for the complex needs of a multicampus environment. Communication across campuses, recognition of common challenges, and the interaction between district functions and campus-based needs are essential. Division of labor and clarity of assignments can only be achieved through careful and thorough communication.

Safety preparations have a priority at MDC that is second to none. We are besieged each year by multiple storms that have the potential to wreak havoc on our campuses and upset the lives of thousands of students and employees. Our approach has been to explore every possible avenue to maximize safety and protect the operations of the college. From that perspective, layers of backup for business operations and IT functioning are standard procedure. Ensuring that multiple and varied communications are available, not only to students and employees regarding storm conditions, but also among various operational personnel to respond to storm conditions, is also essential in confronting the challenges posed by a hurricane.

While a competent, broad-based team is in place to address hurricane needs, the college president is intimately involved in planning during the approach of the storm and in the day-to-day conversations that define the college's response. His attention sets the tone for focus and urgency throughout the institution.

MDC is well schooled by now in hurricane preparation, its response protocols honed in the school of unavoidable experience. We prepare for the inevitable. Each storm and each glancing blow reminds us of the need to remain vigilant. Such are the rigors of paradise.

REFERENCE

Miami Dade College. (2005). Emergency Preparedness Plan. Revised 2005. Miami, FL.

Theodore Levitt is Assistant to the President, Office of the College President, Miami Dade College, Florida.

Chapter 6

Pensacola Junior College Survives Hurricane Ivan

G. Thomas Delaino

II.

Facing the Elements

Pensacola Junior College (PJC) is known for fostering a nurturing learning environment. As an established, learning-centered community college, PJC annually draws more than 30,000 credit and noncredit students. Located in Northwest Florida, PJC primarily serves Escambia and Santa Rosa counties, an area with an estimated population of 450,000. It also reaches into surrounding areas along the Gulf Coast and Southern Alabama. An inherent challenge of the college is its location on the hurricane-prone Gulf Coast. PJC administrators know firsthand that hurricanes can be dangerous killers and that planning ahead reduces the chances of injury and property damage.

PLANNING FOR DISASTER: A TEAM APPROACH

The PJC Emergency Response Team designs and administers a hurricane preparedness/emergency-response plan and holds debriefing sessions to evaluate and implement improvements. The team consists of the president, senior vice president, vice president for student affairs, police chief, and other key administrators.

The PJC plan involves creating a communication process to reach students; securing buildings and infrastructure to reduce damage to the college; preparing buildings to be used as shelters; arranging for fuel, food, supplies, damage assessment, debris removal, and repair equipment; establishing an off-site backup of critical data and the college website; designing a telephone tree with

backup phone numbers to immediately reach personnel in and out of state; and initiating a cooperative, mutual-aid plan with local organizations and other community colleges in Florida and along the Gulf Coast.

PENSACOLA JUNIOR COLLEGE EMERGENCY RESPONSE PLAN

1. **Create a communication process to reach students.**

2. **Secure buildings and infrastructure to reduce damage to the college.**

3. **Prepare buildings to be used as shelters.**

4. **Arrange for fuel, food, supplies, damage assessment, debris removal, and equipment repair.**

5. **Establish an off-site backup of critical data and the college website.**

6. **Design a telephone tree with backup phone numbers to immediately reach personnel in and out of state.**

7. **Initiate a cooperative, mutual-aid plan with local organizations and other community colleges in Florida and along the Gulf Coast.**

DISASTER STRIKES: IVAN VISITS PENSACOLA

On Sept. 16, 2004 – three weeks into the fall semester – Hurricane Ivan pounded the greater Pensacola area. For almost 10 hours, the eastern eye wall of the Category 3 storm pummeled PJC campuses with 130-mile-per-hour winds. The result was dozens of downed trees, destroyed classroom buildings, more than 200 lost desktop computers, and severe water and mold damage to the LRC and many other buildings.

Roof gravel, nails, and dangling tree limbs endangered walkways and parking lots. Surrounded by fallen trees and mounds of debris, two campuses became isolated. Other than sparse foot traffic and the arrival of military helicopters, the Pensacola region remained cut off from the outside world for several long, sweltering days. The Pensacola Regional Airport, rail lines, Interstate 10, and north-south highways closed indefinitely. Cities set curfews. For PJC, classes stopped and the devastation in dollars hit nearly $10 million.

RESPONDING TO THE DISASTER

Management decisions. Some PJC Emergency Response Team members stayed on campus during the storm and some arrived immediately after, including PJC President Tom Delaino who rallied the entire team, which met daily for the next three weeks.

The first gathering addressed damage analysis and control. Transportation personnel also returned to work as soon as possible to repair college vehicles. At the second meeting, the president committed the college to reopening for students three weeks and three days after Ivan and ensured that the semester would not extend beyond its planned ending.

The vice president for academic affairs gathered as many academic administrators as possible. Final-exam week was cancelled in favor of class meetings; faculty scheduled exams as they saw fit. Department heads met with faculty and jointly decided how learning outcomes could still be

achieved. Academic affairs administrators and staff moved a significant number of classes from damaged buildings.

The president made a key decision to pay all faculty and adjuncts for the missed three weeks for two reasons: They were asked to do a great deal of work to revise their academic plans; and without money, they could not recover and survive, meaning PJC could lose many employees who faced the possibility of relocating. Thanks to the PJC Foundation, the college made small, short-term, emergency loans available to employees who did not have ready cash.

The president also decided that students requesting refunds because of the storm would be accommodated for a period of one month after Ivan. A total of 693 students withdrew and received a refund; 653 of those students were authorized to receive a full or partial refund, resulting in more than $233,000 in refunds.

Foundation monies provided grants and loans to students to replace lost school supplies and books, and the college offered mental-health counseling for students. Other community-based agencies later supplied similar counseling services.

PJC's community outreach surfaced in many ways. Its facilities housed the National Guard and volunteer law enforcement officers from outside the area. While this move provided shelter for emergency responders, it also guaranteed an armed presence to better protect the college from looters and other dangers. For instance, the National Guard cutting trees and clearing roads for immediate access sped up the task of clearing debris.

Community partnerships. PJC's Police Department had a strong relationship with the Escambia Emergency Operations Center (EOC) and assigned a liaison to the center during and after the storm. The contact kept PJC administrators aware of area recovery needs and efforts and allowed close cooperation. PJC housed American Red Cross volunteers, National Guard troops, and sheriff's deputies from other communities in college facilities.

The PJC Field House was a designated special-needs shelter. PJC police and staff assisted community volunteers and medical personnel by helping shelter citizens during and after the storm. Working with the EOC, the PJC police liaison contacted local restaurants losing food due to the loss of refrigeration and then arranged to help feed dozens of emergency workers unable to get home for days on end. Once it was back on air, the college public broadcasting station provided the community with news about hurricane recovery, including PJC information.

In all, the college was closed for 21 days. On the designated Monday, classes opened at all three substitutes. It secured four-wheel-drive vehicles to ensure response to the outlying campuses. Safety personnel videotaped the condition of the campuses and buildings before and after the storm to document damage; documentation for insurance claims must be completed prior to any clean-up efforts.

PJC staff generated FEMA-approved time sheets to record hours worked by all personnel on campus during and immediately after Ivan hit. This provided the FEMA documentation required to reimburse PJC for the hours worked. College administration also preapproved purchase requisitions for local contractors to expedite

Safety personnel videotaped the condition of the campuses and buildings before and after the storm to document damage.

campuses and the PJC Downtown Center. To help spread the news, academic affairs arranged for handouts and volunteers to walk the sidewalks and inform students about classes, classroom locations, and other logistics.

Communications. Many of the planned contingencies for communications failed. Newly purchased cell phones stopped working because cell towers were down or lacked generators. Most local television and radio stations were off the air. Individual faculty attempted to contact students via email; however, the reality was most people were in survival mode, and school was not a priority immediately after the hurricane. The college used EOC contacts to reach local media and journalists from nearby Mobile, Alabama, to get out the message. Eventually, the staff could use backup phones and numbers.

College resources needed. Well before the storm, the college identified personnel who needed to stay on campus during and after the storm, along with emergency repairs. The first contractor arrived on the Pensacola campus the day after winds died down.

Police officers identified and checked the safety of all college employees and family members who had taken shelter in college structures and determined when it was safe for them to go outside. Some PJC employees lived on campus for several weeks because their homes were gone – completely wiped out – and emergency housing was extremely difficult to find.

Many grocery stores and restaurants went out of business. Food stored in the PJC Culinary Arts kitchen fed employees who returned to work immediately after the storm, as well as members of the public in our special needs shelter. Before Ivan hit, many police officers filled gas grill propane tanks and became temporary barbecue chefs. A "Clothes Closet" was established for anyone needing to replace clothes and some household items.

LEARNING FROM DISASTER

Without the prior planning and arrangements, PJC would not have recovered and reopened in three weeks. The mutual commitment of faculty and staff to each other and to students was a major factor in recovery.

Positive elements of the emergency plan follow:

- A strong focus on learning outcomes enabled faculty to respond to a shortened semester with minor loss to students.

- Strong relationships and prior arrangements with local contractors prevented additional damage to exposed buildings and helped clear debris, making campuses safe before the public was invited back.

- Strong relationships with emergency services personnel and local volunteer organizations resulted in mutually beneficial outcomes.

- Strong relationships with other community colleges – from as far away as Wisconsin – delivered offers of assistance and aid.

- The telephone tree that included backup and out-of-state numbers enabled us to contact most employees, check on their safety, and inform them of developments.

- The decision to make gasoline available from college pumps to key PJC employees allowed them to report for work.

- Debriefings and emotional support from trained crisis counselors greatly helped employees.

- Having a significant, rainy-day fund enabled the college to pay contractors for critical work, all while dealing with the slow procedures of reinsurers.

- No data was lost. Two of our IT consortium partners mirrored our student-information system, other critical databases, and our website. PJC's website was up and running within a few days of the storm, allowing students and staff who fled the state to check for announcements.

Prior planning does not prevent every problem. We learned:

- Mobile telephones from multiple networks are a necessity, as are generators in certain buildings to allow recharging.

- Faculty need to provide information in syllabi and on websites regarding how students can continue their learning and receive information throughout an emergency.

- The option of moving traditional classes onto the web needs to be increased.

- Refunding student tuition and fees is the compassionate thing to do. However, the resulting loss in fee revenue hampered the college in some ways, including the speed of recovery.

- Never hand over original photos and videos to the first reinsurer. PJC did, and the reinsurer lost it all, forcing us to scramble for copies and photos from employees' personal cameras. Now, the college provides copies and retains originals.

With foresight, planning, and support from the administration, a college can survive a disaster. Our approach helped us deal with a frightening and overwhelming situation and even gave us a reason to celebrate "Survivin' Ivan" with a collegewide barbecue. The PJC community united and worked as a team, choosing to be victors, not victims.

G. Thomas Delaino is President of Pensacola Junior College, Florida.

Chapter 7

Preparation Saves Lives:
An F-3 Tornado Strikes Campus

Warren R. Nichols, T. Clayton Scott, and Eric J. Melcher

Facing the Elements

Volunteer State Community College is a public comprehensive two-year institution serving a 12-county region in northern middle Tennessee. The Tennessee Board of Education approved the establishment of the college on Nashville Pike in Gallatin, Tennessee, in July 1970. Groundbreaking for the first four buildings on the campus was November 5, 1970.

Today, Volunteer State's main campus consists of 16 buildings on 100 acres in Gallatin, about 27 miles northeast of Nashville. The college also has a

Association. In addition to associate degrees, the college also awards technical certificates.

PLANNING FOR DISASTER

Following a variety of college crises across the country, the administration at Volunteer State began a review of its emergency plans in 2003 to guarantee its preparedness when a crisis occurred on campus. They discovered that the college had very minimal

The plans that did exist were rarely practiced with drills to ensure their successful execution.

campus in Livingston, Tennessee, and numerous off-campus operations. When it opened its doors in Fall 1971, enrollment was 581. Enrollment has steadily risen with over 7,300 students enrolled in classes for fall 2006. Since its founding, over 90,000 students have attended the college.

It is accredited by the Commission on Colleges of the Southern Association of Colleges and Schools and holds membership in the American Association of Community Colleges, the Southern Association of Junior Colleges, and the Tennessee College

emergency plans. In addition, the plans that did exist were rarely practiced with drills to ensure their successful execution.

The president implemented a strategy to develop a complete disaster preparedness plan and test it with regular exercises to guarantee success when a crisis struck. The president charged the president's cabinet and Department of Public Safety to create a detailed emergency preparedness plan that would be used in the event of any type of emergency anywhere on campus.

The Department of Public Safety, the president, and the president's cabinet, working in collaboration with local and state emergency management agencies, created an 89-page Emergency Management Plan, publishing it in February 2004. The plan is available in its entirety online at www.volstate.edu/Policies/PublicSafety/VSCC-EmergencyManagement.pdf.

The plan includes sections detailing a crisis operational plan, a crisis communication plan, a crisis response plan, and a crisis recovery plan. It also outlines preparedness plans for campus crises in a variety of scenarios (see Figure A).

In addition, the plan also outlines a schedule for evacuation drills and tornado drills, as well as evaluation criteria for each.

Figure A.
SCENARIOS FOR PREPAREDNESS PLANS FOR CAMPUS CRISES

1. Earthquakes
2. Fire
3. Tornado
4. Explosion on Campus
5. Chemical and Radiation Spills
6. Bomb Threat
7. Cardio-Vascular Emergencies
8. Violent or Criminal Behavior
9. Peaceful, Nonobstructive Demonstrations
10. Nonviolent, Disruptive Demonstrations
11. Violent, Disruptive Demonstrations
12. Psychological Crisis
13. Utility Failure
14. Elevator Malfunction

An essential element of the plan is the role of building coordinators. Building coordinators are volunteers in each of the campus's 16 buildings who oversee the evacuation of the building's occupants or their movement to a safe space inside the building. The coordinators participate in workshops and reviews to ensure their preparedness when a crisis occurs, either in their particular building or elsewhere on campus. The coordinators are issued yellow vests and two-way communication radios.

In January 2006 a small generator fire put the process to the test. A review of the event showed the system did not work as well as it should have. People did not fully obey the building coordinators or properly follow some of the procedures.

The president ordered a review of the system, an increase in campus education, and intensive drills for every building on campus. The training and drills continued for the next several months.

DISASTER STRIKES: THE APRIL 7, 2006, TORNADO

On April 7, 2006, the Emergency Management Plan was severely tested when the campus was hit by an F-3 tornado. The events and actions before, during, and after the tornado are described in the timeline that follows.

Noon. Throughout the day, weather forecasters warn of the possibility of severe weather in and around the middle Tennessee region. Thunderstorms dot the region, bringing with them heavy amounts of rainfall. An assistant vice president heads to the president's office to make him aware of tornado watches and warnings in western Tennessee. The two begin watching television weather coverage as the severe storms move from west Tennessee into the middle Tennessee region.

1:00 p.m. As the storm front moves east, the National Weather Service begins issuing tornado watches and warnings in portions of western middle Tennessee. The front is now a storm front with heavy rains, high winds, and the possibility of tornadoes. Upon hearing of the impending severity of the front, the president notifies Public Safety of the severe weather and the tornado watches and warnings just to the west.

1:05 p.m. Public Safety issues an email warning to all administration, faculty, and staff on campus concerning the approaching storms and their possible severity.

1:30 p.m. As the storms intensify and tornado watches quickly turn to warnings in neighboring counties, administrators begin seriously considering the possibility of a tornado striking the campus. The elements of the Emergency Management Plan are quickly reviewed and implemented.

1:46 p.m. Public Safety addresses the campus about the imminent storms and possible tornado activity over the campuswide intercom system. Building coordinators are notified and a radio check is completed in anticipation of the need for radio use.

1:50 p.m. Building coordinators begin moving building occupants to designated safe spaces and follow up with a room-by-room check for those not aware of the evacuation. Classes are interrupted and students evacuate to safe spaces. Safe spaces include building basements, as well as interior rooms and hallways in buildings that do not have a basement.

2:00 p.m. The National Weather Service issues a Tornado Warning for Sumner County, where the Volunteer State campus lies. The warning is relayed over the campuswide intercom system and over the building coordinators' radios.

2:02 p.m. A tornado is sighted and touches down in Goodlettsville, about 17 miles southwest of campus. Building coordinators do a last-minute, room-by-room check and then join others in safe spaces in their respective buildings. Heavy rains and strong winds hit the campus.

2:23 p.m. As students, administration, faculty, and staff wait in safe spaces, notification of a tornado on campus echoes through the building coordinators' radios. The tornado cut a path northeast from Goodlettsville through the neighboring city of Hendersonville to the Gallatin campus.

The F-3 tornado, with estimated winds of 165-170 miles per hour, first hits and damages the Fox Maintenance Building, then crosses two parking lots, throwing more than 80 cars and trucks in the air before hitting Caudill Hall. Caudill Hall houses the Wemyss Auditorium, along with classrooms, faculty offices, and the campus radio station. The tornado crosses another parking lot and strikes the Ramer Administration Building before heading off campus into neighboring businesses and homes.

THE RESPONSE

2:30 p.m. The immediate search-and-rescue effort is hampered by one big problem: The storms are not over. Other communities are still reporting tornadoes. This is especially serious because of the power outage. Campus police struggle to get the latest weather information. The two most heavily damaged buildings are evacuated to the Wood Campus Center basement. The building coordinators take the opportunity to assess any injuries in their buildings. Information is communicated via the portable radio system, which operates with battery power.

2:45 p.m. Sumner County emergency management volunteers arrive on campus to help with the injury assessment. They do a room-to-room search of the two most heavily damaged buildings.

3:00 p.m. It is determined that there have been only a few minor injuries on campus. These people are actually motorists passing on nearby Nashville Pike who attempted to get into the college to escape the twister. The campus nurse, along with Volunteer State allied health professionals, assist with the triage and assessment. Only one ambulance is needed.

3:00 p.m. The public relations staff checks with emergency responders, building coordinators, and the president to determine the extent of injuries. When they are sure of their facts, they start calls to area television stations. The public relations staff carries media contact lists and other emergency contact information in their briefcases. The message is a simple one: There is major damage on campus, but only minor injuries. Reassuring parents of students and loved ones of faculty and staff is the most important task. Cell phone connection is spotty.

3:40 p.m. The entire campus population is moved to the gym in the Pickel Field House.

3:45 p.m. The PR staff makes another round of calls to all area television stations. They communicate the traffic problems and urge people not to come to campus, once again reassuring people that there are only minor injuries on campus. This information is becoming more important as fatalities are reported in neighborhoods near the campus. One radio station reports that there has been a death on campus. It is quickly corrected as the Associated Press picks up the information from the television phone interviews with the PR staff.

4:00 p.m. A room is set up at the Pickel Field House for an emergency cabinet meeting. The president, vice presidents, deans, and PR staff

informal system of car pooling is set up to ensure that everyone can make it off campus and to their homes.

7:00 p.m. The campus is evacuated and closed. The scope of the storm damage is now apparent: touchdowns in four counties, 12 people dead, dozens injured, dozens of homes destroyed and hundreds damaged. Volunteer State has suffered major structural damage to two buildings and minor damage to almost every building on campus.

THE AFTERMATH

It became apparent almost immediately that the building coordinator system saved lives. Building coordinators directed people to the safe spaces of buildings, did a quick room-to-room assessment to make sure people took cover, and provided invaluable information when the tornado struck. Maintenance staff used the radios to communicate

The public relations staff carries media contact lists and other emergency contact information in their briefcases.

attend. Plans are discussed for immediate reaction and longer-term issues. The primary problem is how to evacuate the campus. Traffic is backed up for miles on Nashville Pike. Police have the road blocked in both directions. The long-term issues involve communication with students about class cancellations. It is apparent that it will take at least several days to reopen the campus. An emergency list of home and cell phone numbers of cabinet members and PR staff is distributed.

4:15 p.m. Students, faculty, and staff work together to bring food and water to the Pickel Field House.

5:30 p.m. The Sumner County Emergency Management Agency orders that the campus be evacuated entirely. They set up routes off campus. More than 80 vehicles have been destroyed by the tornado. Many people have no way to get home. An

that the tornado was on campus, which allowed people to brace themselves for impact, covering their heads and crawling under tables.

The aftermath of the storm proved the most challenging part of the day. The power loss and the communication issues were frustrating, but those challenges were slowly overcome.

Administrators with the Tennessee Board of Regents (TBR) were watching the television coverage of the tornado closely. On hearing news that a tornado had struck Volunteer State, they put into action a disaster response plan. That plan had been refined greatly after a tornado hit the Austin Peay State University campus in Clarksville, Tennessee, in 1999. The lessons learned from that storm were immediately applied to the Volunteer State disaster. Jerry Preston, executive director of Facilities Development, says his staff members were on the phone within an hour of the tornado hitting Volunteer State. They began scheduling clean-up and recovery specialists, roofing contractors, and towing companies to respond to the campus. The president talked with TBR Chancellor Manning and plans were worked out for the response.

That night, as the campus was closing, some companies began to arrive with materials to board up windows. They were directed to leave the materials, since the campus was closed by order of

was on vacation but immediately returned to take up the huge task of moving offices and classrooms.

The power outage lasted five days. During this time, all telephone operations were down and the website was off line. Information technology staff worked to put up a temporary web page with hosting from a sister institution, Middle Tennessee State University. The emergency web page included class cancellation information and daily updates on the progress of clean up and repair. The local media

In all, 11 classrooms and 72 faculty and staff offices had to be relocated.

emergency officials. By early the next morning, dozens of workers from several companies were back at the campus starting the clean up.

The day after the storm was a whirlwind of clean-up efforts and damage assessment. TBR officials, the president, and facilities staff were on the scene at daylight to direct the operation. Tennessee Governor Phil Bredesen toured the campus and, in a darkened conference room, held a meeting with local lawmakers and officials. There was also a deluge of media requests from local and national television, radio, and newspaper outlets. The public relations staff accompanied media on tours of the campus. The governor held a news conference on campus before departing via helicopter.

It was apparent that many classrooms and offices in the two most heavily damaged buildings would not be useable. Space became one of the most important issues. The campus could not reopen for classes until a plan was devised to move classes from damaged classrooms to any available space. The academic affairs administration began searching for available space and coordinating a plan. In all, 11 classrooms and 72 faculty and staff offices had to be relocated. The director of facilities

assisted in getting information out to students, faculty, and staff. Several news releases were sent during the week as new information developed. News media interviews happened many times a day for the entire week, as PR staff worked from cell phones and from home.

Computers had been shut down prior to the storm hitting campus, so no data was lost. The return of power meant that the website could be restored in its usual form. Unfortunately, once the site was working, students thought the campus had reopened. To prevent confusion, the site was immediately returned to the emergency page until the day before classes resumed.

The college was closed for 10 days. One of the days was already scheduled as a holiday, so only four weekday and two weekend class days were lost. The campus reopened for classes on Monday, April 17. Academic affairs administrators put together a chart of changes for the students. Volunteers were posted outside the damaged buildings to point students to the new class locations.

In retrospect, leadership during the storm and its aftermath took many forms. The chief of campus police and the assistant chief were both in Nashville at a scheduled disaster drill. The office supervisor was left in charge of warnings and communications. She was one of many heralded for her efforts during the emergency.

The president worked to set the agenda and map out the immediate and long-term needs. Members of the cabinet took up the initiatives and communicated with the various departments. Homes became work centers. Cell phones and laptops became essential parts of the process. The maintenance and facilities staff had a huge task in the weeks following the storm. Even with the assistance of outside contractors, the staff worked long hours for many days. The business office took a huge hit from the storm. The tornado struck that office with a force that blew out all the windows and ripped off the roof. Documents were scattered across campus. The entire office had to be moved to another building and staff members put in long hours trying to restore the system.

The president worked with the TBR to develop plans for short-term and long-term clean up and rebuilding. Daily meetings were held with contractors to determine the status of work and to project when the campus could reopen for classes.

The tornado caused more than $6 million in damage; the latest total is now approaching $7 million. The college will be responsible for paying between $600,000 and $1 million. The self-insurance the college carries was designed to cover $90 per square foot in replacement costs, but current construction costs are averaging $210 per square foot. The final payments will be made in coordination with the State of Tennessee and the Federal Emergency Management Agency.

LEARNING FROM DISASTER

The emergency drills in the months before the tornado proved to be invaluable. Putting together the building coordinator system was a long process and many people questioned the disruption to the campus. The number of people who approached the president after the storm to specifically credit the

drills for helping save lives was remarkable. The building coordinator system, the radio communications, and the intercom system in each building were also critical tools during the storm. The college is working to refine these efforts. More drills are scheduled, and a meeting of building coordinators was held to assess how the response went and what could be improved.

The president and others at Volunteer State have been asked to make presentations about the tornado and the college response. The audiences have included people from colleges and universities across Tennessee. Their response is a bit surprising. Many say they have not often participated in an emergency drill, while others say they have never participated in such a drill.

While many schools have significant disaster plans, the drills seem to be an aspect that may be getting less attention. Volunteer State had a detailed disaster plan, which was available online and was distributed to leadership posts on campus. However, it was the drills and the building coordinator system that really made the difference. It became clear that the building coordinators needed to practice emergency situations to respond correctly. Moreover, the students, faculty, and staff had to be convinced to take those building coordinators, and in fact the whole emergency response process, seriously. People did take those building coordinators seriously on the day of the tornado, and that response and planning made the difference. Preparation saved lives.

Warren R. Nichols is President; T. Clayton Scott is Assistant Professor of Communications and Journalism; and Eric J. Melcher is Communications and Public Relations Coordinator at Volunteer State Community College, Tennessee.

III.

Perspectives on Handling
Emergency Situations

Chapter 8

Powder to the People

Thomas I. Anderson

III.

Perspectives on
Handling Emergency
Situations

One month after the terrorist attacks of September 11, 2001, Brookhaven College in Farmers Branch, Texas, experienced an emergency situation that arrived on board a Dallas Area Rapid Transit bus that pulled up to the college's stop in front of the student services building.

A little before 7:00 p.m. on October 10, the college police officer in charge received a call from a

police and fire departments were alerted and quickly arrived on campus.

The period following the September 11 attacks was a time during which a number of anthrax scares were alarming the nation. With anthrax being in the forefront, and with the deep uncertainty and widespread suspicion that stemmed from the attacks, the appearance of a white powdery

The appearance of a white powdery substance inside a bus on the campus set into motion a test of the college's safety plan.

bus driver who reported that a passenger had gotten off the bus in front of the school and had left a white, powdery substance on a seat and on the floor. The officer in charge immediately notified the college's chief of police, David Reagan, who had left campus for the day and was on his way home.

Chief Reagan, who was now on his way back to the college, instructed the on-scene police officer to call in two additional police officers. Since the college's president, Alice Villadsen, was out of town, Chief Reagan next notified Vice President Maxine Rogers, the administrator in charge, and other administrators. Rogers would monitor and oversee developments, remaining on the scene until the situation was resolved. The Farmers Branch

substance inside a bus on the campus set into motion a test of the college's safety plan.

"The college had a plan whereby the police and facilities departments would work cooperatively in securing the campus," explained Rogers, the college's vice president of finance at the time. "Facilities would control the traffic while police secured the situation under the direction of the police officer on duty. This is what happened during this incident as the local authorities took charge."

Brookhaven College is one of seven colleges of the Dallas County Community College District. Located in the city of Farmers Branch just north of Dallas, the college serves a mixed student body of Caucasians, African Americans, a fast-growing

Hispanic populace, and international students from over 100 different countries. The college is in a densely populated urban setting with all its attendant advantages and disadvantages, among the latter being the suspicions that can quickly arise

Student Services Center. The Farmers Branch Hazardous Materials Unit, donning their protective suits, entered the bus and removed the questionable powdery substance for testing. These officers also decontaminated the bus. All occupants were

> *Brookhaven's administration, like many entities with responsibility for the safety of others, decided to err on the side of caution if and whenever possible threats arose.*

during tense times, exacerbated by the anonymity that a large population affords.

October 2001 was not a typical fall at this community college of approximately 10,000 credit students. Nerves were frayed and emotions ran deep. Concern for the safety of students and employees was never higher on the college's agenda, and it was not easy to distinguish real threats from chimeras during that period. Brookhaven's administration, like many entities with responsibility for the safety of others, decided to err on the side of caution if and whenever possible threats arose.

The immediate concern surrounding the powdery substance was for the people who were on the bus. They were removed to an isolated area outside but nearby. However, the passenger who had sparked the incident had disappeared after getting off the bus, heading into the campus to classes or activities unknown.

Both college and city police officers set about cordoning off a 300-foot area around the bus. The main entrance to the Student Services Center was locked. Personnel from the college's facilities department directed students around the building during this peak evening time when one set of classes was ending and another beginning, with most students normally passing through the

interviewed and police obtained their vital information. Calm returned after the powdery substance on the bus was determined to be sugar.

After this incident, the college's safety team reviewed the safety plan and its adequacy. Overall, the plan worked.

"We learned that the plan that had been developed worked as far as controlling the college population," said Rogers. "The foot traffic and auto traffic was controlled and information was conveyed in a manner that did not panic the employees and students."

Communication among all relevant personnel was quick and effective. All college administrators had been given a wallet-sized quick-call list that contained all telephone numbers, including cell phone numbers, of all key personnel. This simple, common-sense arrangement proved effective; for example, Chief Reagan was contacted as soon as the incident began to unfold, and he in turn was able to communicate with other necessary personnel to assess the situation and, as the person with primary responsibility for addressing the emergency, issue orders.

Brookhaven College has a concurrent jurisdiction agreement with the Farmers Branch police department. In this particular instance, while the college's police were the first responders, the nature of the scare called for additional personnel and more resources than the college itself could provide. The local police force's hazardous materials unit was essential in defusing this situation through their specially trained officers, equipment, and lab facilities.

While it was reassuring that the college's safety plan was adequate for this particular emergency, this incident proved to be a test case whereby the plan could subsequently be reviewed. One part of the plan that proved inadequate was that the college did not have enough on-duty police officers available during the evening to handle the emergency. Given that early evening is the second-busiest period of the day for in-session classes and the number of students and faculty on the campus, the staffing shortfall proved to be a concern. A related factor is that most of the instructors who are teaching at this time are adjunct faculty who would tend to have limited knowledge not only of college emergency procedures, but of the layout of the campus itself.

"I believe that this incident caused us to reexamine the safety plan for flexibility and realization that you cannot answer all possible emergencies with one plan," observed Villadsen.

"The purpose of the emergency plan is to provide the maximum amount of safety for faculty, staff, students, and visitors," explained Reagan. "More definitive guidelines were written to update the emergency response plan." Reagan also explained that after the attacks of September 11, 2001, efforts were undertaken by the federal government to assist local entities in emergency preparedness, for example, guidelines concerning the handling of mail were implemented in the college's mailroom.

So what was learned from this incident at Brookhaven College that could be applied to other community colleges? "I think one discovery with this incident was that we had not given sufficient attention to a lock-down or 'hold where you are' mode," commented Villadsen. "The incident was one in which we needed to keep anyone from leaving campus until the [substance] could be identified. How do you lock down a college? Did the safety plan include that alternative? How do you get word to all classes that they should stay put?"

Villadsen offered some useful principles that emerged from Brookhaven's experience that could be applied by any community college building a safety plan, including determining key personnel and communications and at least two additional levels of chief operatives in emergencies; deciding which emergency agencies and contacts are to be notified and having phone numbers accessible; training police officers in hazards; and determining types of campus communications about emergencies, e.g. bells, signals, or bullhorns.

PRINCIPLES FOR EMERGENCY PREPAREDNESS IDENTIFIED BY VILLADSEN

1. Determine key personnel and communications, plus two additional levels of chief operatives in emergencies.

2. Decide which emergency agencies and contacts are to be notified and have phone numbers accessible

3. Train police officers in hazards

4. Determine types of campus communications about emergencies, e.g., bells, signals, bullhorns.

5. Don't wait until a situation occurs to develop a plan.

6. Identify an authorized spokesperson for the college and the process for gathering information and formulating a press release.

"Don't wait until a situation occurs to develop a plan," advised Rogers. "Two very important points are to control the situation without escalation and control the outflow of information. Identify…the authorized spokesperson for the college and the process for gathering the information and formulating the press release. What you want to do is provide facts and what you don't want is

safety, and risk, and making recommendations for corrective or preventive actions.

"At Brookhaven College, we take safety seriously," commented the college's current president, Sharon Blackman. "We must be prepared as best we can for any emergency situation that arises. These are anxious times, and we need to expect more crisis situations. As situations arise, we

Brookhaven College's safety plan is regularly reviewed and updated by the college's Safety and Loss Prevention Team.

different versions of the same story."

Brookhaven College's safety plan attempts to provide focused and flexible guidelines that will assist the college with any emergency. It is regularly reviewed and updated by the college's Safety and Loss Prevention Team, whose charge includes reviewing issues related to the environment, health,

have to be quick, focused, skillful, and effective with our response."

Thomas I. Anderson is Assistant to the Vice President of Instruction at Brookhaven College, Dallas County Community College District, Texas.

Chapter 9
Coping With the Murder of a Colleague on Campus

Jackson N. Sasser

III.

Perspectives on Handling Emergency Situations

Santa Fe Community College (SFCC) is a multicampus, comprehensive community college located in Gainesville, Florida. In January, 2002, I became the college's fourth president. Approximately 70 percent of 16,000 SFCC students are enrolled in programs typically taken to transfer to the nearby University of Florida. The college has

diverse skills including counselors to give advice and comfort. During the fall and late summer of 2004, the college used its crisis management team during two hurricanes and had several controversies that did not require the ICS but did necessitate exhaustive internal and external communications strategies.

> *When there are crises that affect individuals personally and emotionally, the college calls in its trauma response team, a group of staff members with diverse skills.*

an array of services to serve students at all levels of academic preparation, including an Employment Training Center to assist disadvantaged students in school and finding employment.

The college uses an incident management system (ICS) adapted to a higher education setting. The ICS is a component of the National Incident Management System (NIMS). The college's crisis management team (CMT) conducts frequent tabletop drills under this system to practice responses to a variety of hypothetical crises. When there are crises that affect individuals personally and emotionally, the college calls in its trauma response team, a group of staff members with

EMERGENCY SITUATION

The tragedy began at SFCC the morning of October 27, 2004. Denise White, a contracted temporary employee in SFCC's Employment Training Center for approximately three months, was stabbed in her office on the college's Northwest, or main, campus, by a man identified by witnesses as her estranged husband, Samuel White. She died in the hospital less than two hours later. At the time of the murder, I was on a plane to Atlanta en route to a League for Innovation in the Community College board meeting at Kirkwood Community College.

Mrs. White counseled at-risk students, many on welfare, by regularly checking with and advising them about academic progress and employment plans. The murder occurred in the presence of at least three co-workers and was heard by several others. Employees tried to stop Mr. White from assaulting his wife and then from fleeing, to no

Governor, and the Chancellor of Community Colleges and Workforce Education, and prepared an email message to the college community that was also posted on our internet home page. I had complete confidence in the ability of my staff to manage this crisis; indeed, they did so under the leadership of our vice presidents for academic affairs

By prearrangement for this kind of tragedy, counselors from the county crisis center arrived to assist.

avail. Mr. White was followed by an employee as he ran from the crime scene. Descriptions of the assailant and his car and license number were provided to law enforcement. He fled before the arrival of SFCC police, who secured the scene. Assistance was quickly forthcoming from the local sheriff's office. All appropriate outside law enforcement agencies were contacted.

According to the local state attorney, at Mrs. White's request a restraining order had been issued against her husband, who had been charged with two counts of domestic battery a few months earlier. Mrs. White had not informed anyone at the college about the restraining order or charges. The couple was scheduled to attend a court hearing the day after the murder to resolve an ongoing custody dispute about their four children.

Based on information provided by witnesses, Mr. White was apprehended the next day in Virginia and extradited two weeks later to the local sheriff's office, where he was charged with first-degree murder.

ORGANIZATIONAL RESPONSE

When I arrived in Atlanta, my executive assistant contacted me by cell phone and I immediately made arrangements to return to Gainesville. I contacted the college's District Board of Trustees, Florida's

and student affairs. However, I felt I needed to be present, and I assumed direct leadership upon arrival at the college in the afternoon.

Part of the college's crisis management team gathered in a room adjacent to the secured murder scene. Part of the CMT set up headquarters in its accustomed location in the building next door. The coordinator of the college's counseling center went to the hospital to be with Mrs. White and her family.

Law enforcement immediately located the Whites' children and placed them in protective custody. Temp Force, Mrs. White's employer, was immediately contacted.

Employees in the vicinity of the murder were moved to a nearby campus location to be interviewed as witnesses by police. When they were released, administrative leave was granted to those most directly affected by the crime. The SFCC counseling center coordinated counseling for employees and students.

In short order, the sheriff's office, with its greater resources, assumed responsibility for the law enforcement aspect of the case. By prearrangement for this kind of tragedy, counselors from the county crisis center arrived to assist.

The campus was informed that it was to direct media inquiries to the SFCC public information office (PIO) to ensure that a consistent message of concern and competency would be given by the college. The PIO sent an email notice to all departments, faculty, and staff about the incident, that students and employees were safe, and that classes and services would continue as scheduled. A briefer statement was prepared for the college switchboard. Periodic emails from me to college employees followed. The PIO was present at the crime scene to facilitate the media.

The PIO informed the media that Mrs. White's hiring, salary, and benefits were arranged by Temp

colleague, is not typically addressed in practice exercises. It must be considered, particularly by the chief executive. I returned to campus that afternoon and as soon as possible visited employees most affected by the crime. College counselors from the trauma response team were made available and counseled employees upon request.

We were respectful of Mrs. White's family, friends, colleagues, and the entire college community. I wrote a letter to the Santa Fe family, as we often refer to ourselves, to share and give

It is self-evident but bears emphasis that preparation and practice are essential to ensure an organized and effective response.

Force, an independent contractor, not the human resources department of the college. This distinction did not affect the college's response to the tragedy but made clear that certain inquiries could be made only to Temp Force.

LEARNING FROM TRAGEDY

The college safety plan was effective for two reasons: our police chief, Daryl Johnston, led the development of a plan suitable for education in general and Santa Fe in particular; and Johnston schedules crisis tabletops with the management team at least twice a year. It is self-evident but bears emphasis that preparation and practice are essential to ensure an organized and effective response.

Communications are inevitably a problem in any crisis. A simple but effective expedient is to distribute laminated wallet cards with the cell phone numbers of key crisis management personnel. Often, some of those personnel are on the site of the crisis, off campus, or at the crisis headquarters.

The emotional and psychological aftermath of a crisis, particularly a tragedy involving the loss of a

expression to its feelings. The letter also informed that we would offer an informal seminar on the subject of domestic violence, that employees could contribute to a fund on behalf of Mrs. White's children, that the college has a standing offer of a scholarship to each of the children, and that anyone was welcome to add flowers, stuffed animals, photographs, and the like at a temporary memorial in front of the college.

In consultation with family members and colleagues, the college chose a tree planting ceremony to establish a living memorial for Mrs. White. The ceremony was brief. After thinking about how she devoted her life to others whose circumstances mirrored her modest beginnings, I concluded my remarks with part of a poem by William Blake:

> Love seeks not itself to please
>
> Nor for itself has any care
>
> But to others it gives its ease
>
> And builds a Heaven in Hell's despair.

Jackson N. Sasser is President of Santa Fe Community College, Florida.

Chapter 10

After-Hours Crisis Management

Ann Brand

Perspectives on Handling Emergency Situations

St. Louis Community College at Florissant Valley is located on 110 tree-lined acres in suburban North St. Louis County, Missouri. It includes 12 campus buildings and two substantial ponds, one surrounded by natural Missouri grasses and vegetation.

Florissant Valley is valued by area residents not only for its educational mission, but also as the community's park. From dawn to dusk, community walkers and joggers can be seen on the college

enrollments of more than 6,000 credit students per semester, plus continuing education and other visitors, the most serious issues have been car or equipment thefts. Since September 11, 2001, though, we all are well aware of how quickly the comfort level on campuses can change.

Our test came late one Friday afternoon in October 2005. Visitors on campus reported what appeared to be a body floating in a pond. Campus police called the local fire department, which

> ## We were well aware, however, that rumors would be rampant as staff and students heard reports second- or third-hand.

perimeter. It's not unusual for residents to use our tennis courts and track areas, or just be on campus to admire the scenery.

Such openness carries responsibilities. Walking tracks are designated, trees and bushes trimmed, and the campus is well lighted. Police patrol on foot, by car, and with bicycles. Campus leadership has made every effort to ensure an open, but safe and secure environment. In addition, the campus police chief is a well-liked, well-respected partner with area city and county police departments.

Throughout its 45 year history, Florissant Valley has had very few crime incidents. Despite

retrieved the body of an unidentified female. The local police also were summoned, and because of the nature of the crime, it was decided that the local police department's Crime Scene Investigators (CSI) would be the lead investigatory agent after determining at the scene that there were no signs of foul play. Campus staff aided in the investigation and handled media contact.

This all took place leading into the weekend. Most of the full-time staff was gone, and information was very sketchy over the weekend. We were well aware, however, that rumors would be rampant as staff and students heard reports second- or third-hand, and became aware of sketchy media reports.

Friday afternoon, the Florissant Valley president updated the chancellor and called the campus leadership team with what we knew – very little at that time. A cabinet meeting was scheduled early Monday morning, when we knew we would have more information and a better reading of what was being said.

An important element of our information campaign was our student newspaper. We met several times with the students and enlisted their support in helping provide accurate information. They were terrific; the student reporters realized that inaccurate or sensational information would hurt the college's reputation and image. Their articles reassured students who were still getting garbled messages.

We met several times with the students and enlisted their support in helping provide accurate information.

By Monday, police had identified the victim, a former student, and further determined no foul play was involved. This satisfied the external media, but the campus grapevine was buzzing. Rumors ranged from "cover-up" to "drug deal gone bad." Some believed the victim was a current student, and many day staff, unaware until Monday that anything had occurred, were troubled by the rumors of the incident. Students and some parents started calling the campus for clarification.

Florissant Valley has a tradition of providing clear, open information to staff about issues. Campus leadership decided to follow this model to give students and staff the opportunity to hear the truth about the incident and ask questions about any concerns or rumors they may have heard. Two all-campus forums were scheduled Monday for staff and students. The Florissant Valley president provided background and explained why we were scheduling these forums. We relied on our campus police chief to describe the incident and explain what the investigation had found. At the end of the forums, we distributed a statement that could be used by faculty and staff to answer questions by students or other staff. Similar information was provided to those staff who worked evenings.

The investigation took several weeks to complete. Over time we updated staff with appropriate information. Although there are always folks ready to see conspiracies, most staff and students believed the information we provided.

I believe our approach was successful because the campus president has a history of honesty and openness with staff. Trust takes time to earn, and we never squander an opportunity. In addition to asking staff and students to believe our statement – the victim was not a student; she was not the victim

- Include internal and external components in the crisis communication plan.
- Involve student reporters in the crisis communication plan.
- Provide adequate information to evening and part-time staff.
- Recognize the vulnerability people can feel in light of an unexplained death on campus.

of foul play; the incident was unique; no one else on campus was involved nor should anyone feel unsafe – we continually updated information and

media than to handle rumors. Make good use of your student reporters, and don't cut them out. Also, don't short-change information to evening

Never underestimate how vulnerable people can feel in light of an unexplained death on campus.

continued to stress that our campus was a safe and secure place to learn.

As we reviewed this incident, several things stood out: It's critical to have an internal, as well as external component to the crisis communication plan. Perhaps even more so, since most public relations practitioners know how to deal with major media, but the culture, sensibilities, and communication styles of our own staff can be more difficult to gauge. Often it's easier to deal with

and part-time staff. They are less familiar with leadership staff and communications plans. Finally, never underestimate how vulnerable people can feel in light of an unexplained death on campus. We had some very jittery students and staff, and we continued our strong police presence and information campaign until all issues were resolved.

Ann Brand serves in Community Relations at St. Louis Community College at Florissant Valley, Missouri.

Preparing for the Worst

Chapter 11

Community Colleges as Emergency Shelters: The Alabama Plan

Alice W. Villadsen

Preparing for the Worst

Colleges throughout the nation have often been included within community emergency and evacuation plans. For instance, Lee College in Baytown, Texas, became a short-term evacuation site for those fleeing hurricane Katrina in Louisiana, and Faulkner State College in Bay Minette, Alabama, served in a similar capacity for area

public community colleges in Alabama are within one state system, the entire system can be a unified emergency resource for the entire state.

The State of Alabama and its coastline suffered through two massive hurricanes in successive years: Ivan in 2004 and Katrina in 2005. In previous years, the state had experienced seemingly more than its

An innovative state emergency plan has been developed that uses the state's community colleges in a coordinated way as evacuation centers.

evacuees. Sometimes colleges are listed as logical evacuation sites for local K-12 schools should an emergency hit the community's public schools. Community college campuses are at times used as practice sites for city emergency organizations. Brookhaven College in Dallas has seen helicopters, ambulances, and fire trucks use its grounds to rehearse emergency situations resulting from simulated explosions, fires, and pandemics. However, most of these situations involve one college working cooperatively with another college or with an area hospital or other emergency-related local agency. Not so in Alabama, where an innovative state emergency plan has been developed that uses the state's community colleges in a coordinated way as evacuation centers. Since all

share of the monster storms. Tornadoes spawned by hurricanes also have caused significant damage, and rising water and floods have happened in the aftermath of these hurricanes.

Alabama contains two Gulf Coast counties – Mobile and Baldwin – that are highly vulnerable to hurricane landfalls, and several southern counties that are often in the pathway of hurricanes moving northward from Alabama, Florida, or Mississippi. Hurricane Katrina wrecked the New Orleans area in Louisiana and southern coastline Mississippi, but the small towns dotting the western shores of Mobile Bay in Alabama also sustained massive damage. In 2004, Hurricane Ivan did enormous damage to Gulf Shores, Dauphin Island, and the Mobile and Baldwin areas generally.

RATIONALE FOR THE DEVELOPMENT OF THE PLAN

Because of the breadth and depth of damage and loss of life sustained in Alabama through Ivan and Katrina, Governor Bob Riley determined that a state response plan was necessary as an aid to the usual Red Cross and State Emergency Management responses. Thus, following the destructive summer of 2005, he commissioned a group to examine the possibility of using the state's community colleges as temporary emergency shelters to supplement the usual Red Cross shelters when needed for evacuees living along Alabama's coastlines. The Red Cross is the organization charged by the United States Congress to provide disaster services, initially authorized in 1905 and reaffirmed in federal law in the 1974 Disaster Relief Act and in the 1988 Robert T. Stafford Disaster Relief and Emergency Assistance Act. In response to Governor Riley's request, on June 1, 2006, the Alabama state plan was presented to the governor; it was approved and has been implemented.

KEY PARTNERS

The Alabama College System – the state's two-year college system – partnered with the American Red Cross to certify two-year college facilities as Hurricane Evacuation Centers. As a result of the state's effort, 23 system colleges with 36 certified

sheltering and feeding process. A thorough memorandum of understanding delineates all responsibilities. Adopted within the memorandum of understanding is the Red Cross definition of disaster:

A disaster is a threatening or occurring event of such destructive magnitude and force as to dislocate people, separate family members, damage or destroy homes, and injure or kill people. A disaster produces a range and level of immediate suffering and basic human needs that cannot be promptly or adequately addressed by the affected people, and impedes them from initiating and proceeding with their recovery efforts. National disasters include floods, tornadoes, hurricanes, typhoons, winter storms, tsunamis, hail storms, wildfires, wind storms, epidemics, and earthquakes. Human-caused disasters – whether intentional or unintentional – include residential fires, building collapses, transportation accidents, hazardous materials releases, explosions, and domestic acts of terrorism. (American Red Cross Foundations of Disaster Services Series, July 2003)

In the event of a named storm with a projected strike zone on the Gulf Coast affecting Alabama, all of the colleges review the plan, ensure that they are in readiness based upon checklists of materials and actions included in the plan, and await a possible call from the system chancellor. Should evacuation

As a result of the state's effort, 23 system colleges with 36 certified sites will be able to shelter 22,000 people.

sites will be able to shelter 22,000 people. In addition, four colleges are in the process of being designated as Red Cross Certified Medical Needs shelters. These special needs shelters will be co-located with college evacuation shelters. Following careful planning, it was agreed that the college presidents would manage the college facilities and the Red Cross would manage the

be declared by the Alabama Emergency Operations Center as a result of the impending storm, the governor declares a state of emergency and notifies the community college system chancellor who notifies the appropriate colleges for action. Levels of preparation and action include (1) stand by, (2) alert, (3) activated, and (4) post-landfall. Each action level includes precise action for the colleges to take.

BASICS OF THE STATE PLAN

The state has been divided into three tiers of shelters: Tier 1 is the southern part of the state and consists of eight colleges with 13 sites certified to shelter 5,000; Tier 2 is the middle part of the state and consists of seven colleges with 11 certified sites sheltering over 5,600; and Tier 3, in north Alabama, includes eight colleges with 12 sites and a capacity of 10,200 evacuees. Secondarily, there are three additional colleges not certified but available as secondary shelters if needed.

Community colleges were selected to be certified shelters based on their locations near evacuation routes within the state; however, the plan includes the likelihood that evacuees from neighboring states will also have access to the

COLLEGES' RESPONSIBILITIES

The local colleges are responsible for ensuring that shelters are safe and operational. They provide security services, first responder and first aid, janitorial services, maintenance, and if available, food service. If food service is not available, the Red Cross provides prepackaged meals. The Red Cross will have equipment and supplies stored and distributed to the college shelters in each tier at the appropriate times.

RED CROSS RESPONSIBILITIES

The Red Cross maintains a special liaison to the Alabama state plan and the Alabama College System, and the system also has named a special

Local colleges also can provide transportation for those who need to be evacuated but have no personal means of transportation.

shelters since coastal residents must flee to logical locations not necessarily within their own state boundaries. The tiered categorization of the shelters allows for three levels of response based upon the strength of the hurricane. For Category 1, 2, and 3 hurricanes, the Tier 1 shelters will be opened; for Category 4 storms, Tiers 1 and 2 are activated; and for a Category 5 hurricane, all tiers will be activated.

Not only are the colleges set to receive evacuees who arrive at their locations prior to storms, but local colleges also can provide transportation for those who need to be evacuated but have no personal means of transportation. Through the use of 40 college buses and 66 vans, 2,500 people can be transported at a time. Buses and vans are also designated to move evacuees from one shelter to another if capacity is reached at the first shelter.

liaison to the Red Cross. Red Cross offers specialists to consult with the system at no cost on program planning, shelter identification and management, and emergency operations. Applicable training for system employees in mass care, shelter operations, and appropriate health services in support of shelters is provided as well. Red Cross plans to provide the appropriate volunteers to operate the shelters but may enlist, for up to 14 days, employees of the system colleges to aid in volunteer shelter assignments if needed.

ADDITIONAL ELEMENTS WITHIN THE PLAN

The Alabama Hurricane Preparedness Report includes details describing each of the 36 sites that have been certified by the Red Cross. Such items as evacuee capacity; transportation, including buses and vans; generators; numbers of toilets, sinks, and showers; food preparation areas; dining and seating capacity; laundry facilities; level of health and first aid available; and accessibility are included for each designated college. Utility providers and names and contact information for key employees at each college are also included. Within the report are

The Alabama College System Hurricane Preparedness Plan and Report is evidence that a state, vulnerable to particular disasters – in this case hurricanes – can thoughtfully and thoroughly evaluate its resources; develop a strong partnership with government and an emergency agency, the Red Cross; and prepare for caring for thousands of its

An annual review and evaluation of the plan is required.

scenarios developed and based upon actual hurricanes affecting the state in recent years, along with a detailed state level budget including an emergency shelter needs list. An annual review and evaluation of the plan is required, and the current memorandum of understanding is in effect for three years with the possibility of the plan being reactivated at the conclusion of the cycle.

citizens in case of a severe emergency. With the recent events that have taxed the nation's usual emergency preparedness providers, community colleges in Alabama have proved ready to do their part in protecting the lives of those who need shelter.

Alice W. Villadsen is President Emeritus, Brookhaven College, Dallas County Community College, Texas.

Chapter 12

Creating and Sustaining a Campus Emergency Management Plan That Works

R. Thomas Flynn and Lee E. Struble

Preparing for the Worst

On the morning of September 11, 2001, Monroe Community College administrators activated the campus emergency management plan that was developed in collaboration with police, fire, and other response agencies. The college immediately began gathering data to determine the appropriate and safe course of action for the campus in the aftermath of the terrorist attacks at the World Trade Centers and the Pentagon building, and aboard United Airlines flight 93 in rural eastern Pennsylvania. It was soon learned that several domestic U.S. flights were in the process of being rerouted to the Greater Rochester International Airport. With the knowledge that MCC lies in the direct air path of the airport, it was determined that the most prudent course of action for the college was to evacuate the campus. This decision was supported by the Monroe County officials, who were quickly deployed at the county Emergency Operations Center (EOC) located at the college's Criminal Justice Training Center. The evacuation plan was mobilized and the campus population of over 12,000 students, faculty, staff, and visitors was evacuated in an orderly manner within two hours.

The evacuation involved the coordinated effort of several college departments and outside agencies. The Rochester Transit System was requested to send 10 buses to the campus to initiate the process. The Monroe County Sheriff's Department and Brighton Police Department were dispatched to meet with officials from the Public Safety Department to help coordinate and assist with critical traffic control on all major arteries

from the campus. The MCC public relations staff prepared an official statement with specific evacuation instructions and department volunteers began delivering the prepared statement to each classroom. The MCC home page and voice messaging system were updated with the college closing announcement. Students were instructed to evacuate first, followed by the faculty. Administrators and staff in essential function departments were asked to remain on campus until officially notified otherwise. Upon full evacuation, Public Safety conducted a lockdown of all campus exterior doors and the entrances to the campus were closed. Our emergency management plan had worked.

College administrators across the United States were likewise thrust into rapid implementation of their respective emergency preparedness plans on September 11, 2001. The levels of deployment were relative to the direct impact the tragic events of that day had on the local emergency responding agencies and the immediate life safety concerns of our respective campus communities. While many campuses were able to affirm a sound and efficient plan, others struggled to grapple with how to respond to the fast-moving events of that infamous day.

The widespread devastation and lengthy recovery from Hurricanes Katrina and Rita in 2005 reminded us once again of the vital importance of having an all-hazards emergency preparedness plan for our respective campuses. Katrina and Rita also demonstrated the critical importance of a comprehensive business continuity and contingency plan.

The purpose of this chapter is to share the evolution of our MCC emergency management plan and to relate how we were able to effectively access and use myriad available resources to ensure that our emergency plans are sufficient to meet the daunting task of preparing our campuses for the escalating number of potential crises that we may encounter, ranging from a campuswide power outage or crippling communications shutdown to the widespread implications of a pending pandemic crisis. As we share our experiences in emergency preparedness, we are hopeful you will be able to assess your existing plan and be able to implement some of these suggested strategies to better your respective planning, response, and return-to-business strategies.

The MCC emergency management plan that was put into action on September 11, 2001, is still very similar to the plan in use today. The main reason for the success of our plan was the college's longtime commitment to the emergency preparedness plan of the Public Safety Department and the early adaptation of the incident command system used by local fire departments. This incident command system uses the same principles of incident command that the new presidential directives have mandated of all federal response entities. Adapting, refining, and practicing the emergency management plan and incident command system prepared MCC to execute a well-coordinated and effective response to the events that unfolded on September 11, 2001.

The plan in use today is annually reviewed, revised, and practiced to ensure that all potential participants are fully familiar and proficient in their respective tasks, and that all emergency information is updated and accurate. The plan incorporates all the federally mandated National Incident Management System (NIMS) training and Incident Command System (ICS) training. The ICS training is currently being rolled out by the International Association of Campus Law Enforcement

Administrators (IACLEA) through a Homeland Security grant.

The NIMS requirements were established as a result of the Homeland Security Presidential Directive (HSPD-5) that was issued on February 28, 2003, by President Bush. The purpose of HSPD-5 is to enhance the ability of the United States to manage domestic incidents by establishing a comprehensive national system of incident management. Included within this NIMS requirement is that each campus must adopt, understand, exercise, and train on all the elements of the ICS and the concept of Unified Command (UC) when responding to local, state, or regional crisis. The creation and adoption of this National Response Plan (NRP) outlines how the nation as a whole will plan for and respond to Incidents of National Significance (INS) on a national, state, and local level.

THE SIX COMPONENTS OF NIMS

1. Command and Management
2. Preparedness
3. Resource Management
4. Communications and Information Management
5. Support Technologies
6. Ongoing Management and Maintenance

The National Incident Management System was designed to provide a consistent nationwide approach for federal, state, and local governments to work effectively and efficiently to prepare, prevent, respond to, and recover from domestic incidents, regardless of their cause, size, or complexity. There are six components in NIMS: command and management, preparedness, resource management, communications and information management, support technologies, and ongoing management and maintenance. NIMS has also established a uniform set of processes, protocols, and procedures that all emergency responders, at every level of government, are required to incorporate into their existing plans. Included in these protocols are

- Standardized organizational structures, processes, and procedures;

- Standards for planning, training and exercising, and personnel qualification;

- Equipment acquisition and certification standards;

- Interoperable communications processes, procedures, and systems;

- Information management systems; and

- Supporting technologies, including voice and data communications systems, information systems, and data display systems and specialized technologies.

In order to be fully NIMS compliant, each college or university must first identify the individuals on campus who are required to complete the various NIMS training modules. All designated first responders are required to complete the FEMA IS-700 and ICS-100 courses. These courses

IS-700, ICS-100, ICS-200, and FEMA IS-800. Each course requires approximately one to two hours to complete. The third aspect of NIMS compliance is to ensure that all existing emergency preparedness plans and procedures have fully integrated with NIMS and NRP.

MCC was instrumental in the original design of the ICS training curriculum with the Rochester-based firm, BowMac Educational Services. BowMac has been delivering emergency preparedness training courses internationally for over 20 years, and has enjoyed a close relationship with Monroe Community College and the MCC Regional Police Training Center. In the late 1990s, MCC began working closely with BowMac to enhance the course curriculums and to modify the tabletop exercise simulators used in the college's incident command training program. MCC and the Rochester Institute of Technology (RIT) were also selected as the pilot sites for the "REDI for Campus Emergencies" software program that provides online guides to assist in emergency planning implementation. Plans were written, reviewed, and tested with MCC and RIT project teams prior to being programmed and ported to a web configuration.

When the BowMac Incident Command System training became certified by the DHS Preparedness

The college's comprehensive plan must be consistent with and closely linked to town, county, and state emergency preparedness plans.

can be completed online at www.fema.gov/nims, and course completion certificates are mailed upon successful completion of all courses. In addition to FEMA IS-700 and ICS-100, first-line supervisors are also required to complete ICS-200. All designated command and general staff must complete FEMA

Directorate, it allowed IACLEA to qualify for federal terrorism funding that made this training available to colleges and universities throughout the United States. There are three levels of certified ICS courses offered: Simulation-Based Training for Command Post Personnel; Simulation-Based Training for Initial

Response Personnel; and Simulation-Based Training for Dispatch Personnel. Each course is a three-day, hands-on training program.

The Monroe Community College emergency management plan recognizes that there is a significant responsibility to manage emergency and disaster situations on campus, as well as to

body for weeks or months. Therefore, the plan must be flexible enough to properly manage a wide array of potential responses.

Prevention, mitigation, planning, response, and recovery are all acknowledged as basic elements of effective emergency management. By addressing all of these elements in your plan, you will be able to

The plan must be flexible enough to properly manage a wide array of potential responses.

coordinate with other public safety and local governmental entities and officials when emergencies expand beyond the campus. It is further recognized that the college's comprehensive plan must be consistent with and closely linked to town, county, and state emergency preparedness plans. Therefore, MCC has solicited representation and approval of our emergency management plan at each of these respective governmental levels. A complete risk assessment of potential hazards that could affect our campus and the existing on- and off-campus response capabilities was also an important prerequisite to the development of our plan. This interagency and interdisciplinary cooperation has further enhanced the working relationship between MCC and the many emergency response agencies that we work with to complete this process.

One of the basic concepts of emergency management planning is that the plan should address all hazards. Experience has shown that the only predictability factor in emergency planning is that most emergencies are totally unpredictable. Our ability to respond to the emergency will require a great deal of crisis management, even with the best developed plans. An unforeseen power outage can cripple a campus for days or weeks, or the effects of a natural disaster – e.g., hurricane, ice storm, flood – can displace a residential student

lessen the intensity and duration of any unusual event on your campus. The MCC all-hazard plan is a comprehensive approach. When an incident occurs, it passes through four distinct phases that require management. The MCC plan outlines specific responsibilities for each of the following four phases: (1) crisis; (2) scene management; (3) executive management; and (4) termination and recovery.

The MCC Plan assigns responsibilities for emergency management to existing MCC departments. The assignments are made within the framework of the existing management and organizational structures of the various divisions and departments. Each department on campus must also maintain its own standard operating procedures that are designed to support the overall campus plan. Using existing organizational lines of reporting and authority is also the most productive means to integrate and comply with the federal NIMS directives. The MCC plan allows for each incident to be classified into one of four categories:

- Level 0. Nonemergency/Administrative/ Special Events
- Level I. Monitor/Standby
- Level II. Emergency
- Level III. Disaster

Preparing for the Worst

Certain automatic actions are initiated based upon the incident classification. It is also recognized that for an emergency plan to be successful, first responders must have the training and authority to activate the response plan and initiate critical actions to examine and manage the situation. This is becoming increasingly important as active-shooter protocols are being examined more closely in light of the continued school shootings across the United States.

The decisions that are made, or not made, during the first 30 to 60 minutes of a critical incident – i.e., mass casualty incident, active shooter, hazardous materials incident, or major fire – are crucial to its eventual outcome. The ability to

processing the stress. The Incident Command System training provides a module on critical incident stress to educate the first responders to recognize the symptoms of acute and delayed stress, and to learn how to effectively mitigate stress before, during, and after an incident. As leaders of our respective campuses, it is vitally important that we take care of our first responders, and provide the training and resources necessary to protect our campuses at large.

At MCC, all public safety officers are graduates of MCC's Public Safety Training Center, which trains all recruits in the concepts of the Incident Command System. All MCC officers and selected local law enforcement and emergency response

It is vitally important that we take care of our first responders, and provide the training and resources necessary to protect our campuses at large.

recognize the dangers and to contain the scene rests directly on the initial officers who arrive on the scene. As a result of the potentially serious consequences that can arise from such an event, every security or police officer should be properly trained in scene management. Given the lack of frequency of these major events, it is imperative that Public Safety or Police Departments invest in the training necessary to manage emotionally charged events.

One of the most commonly overlooked aspects of an incident response is the critical incident stress that affects the first-responder professionals who are on the front line. It is a difficult task to recognize and respond to critical incident stress in others, as well as in ourselves. Members of the emergency response field have tried to deal with critical incident stress by either suppressing the stress or

personnel also complete the three-day BowMac course on initial response and scene management. This training allows all participants to manage various types of incidents in a simulated high-stress environment on the model campus simulator.

The core curriculum of the ICS training is the "seven critical tasks" that all first responders must use during the crisis stage of an incident. It is important that all participants in the campus Emergency Management Plan are aware of the implementation of these seven critical tasks as they begin to arrive on the scene of a critical incident. The seven critical tasks are: establish control and communication; identify the "hot zone" (a.k.a. the "kill zone"); establish the inner perimeter; establish the outer perimeter; establish the on-scene command post; establish a staging area; and identify and request additional resources. All of these tasks are expounded upon during the ICS classroom and online training and proficiency are demonstrated in the simulation exercises.

Another important aspect of campus preparedness is the awareness, education, and training of the campus community in the emergency management plan. The MCC plan has been accessible on the college's web page for many years. A comprehensive "Employee Training for Emergency Response" PowerPoint program is also available on the public safety web page. This program serves as a self-tutorial on the common terminology and command structure of an ICS response and provides an overview of the MCC emergency management plan. It also describes the appropriate initial actions and general response options for all personnel to take in the event of a critical incident on campus. Response guides can be printed out for future reference.

MCC also has a very active College Emergency Response Team (CERT) that is comprised of community-minded college employees who volunteer their time to Monroe County and MCC if called upon during an emergency. The team can be used to assist in crowd control during emergency evacuations, provide fixed-post personnel on the perimeter of an emergency, render minor first aid

assistance, or provide any other duties as assigned by the incident commander or designee. All volunteers received 40 hours of formal training at the Public Safety Training Center. There are currently 25 active CERT members on the MCC campus.

If your campus has not adopted the Incident Command System, you need to do so. If you have not become compliant with the new National Incident Management System, you need to do so. MCC's plan is only as good as the training and resources that are committed to support it. If you have not provided the training or resources necessary to implement your campus emergency management plan, you need to do so. Our ability to appropriately respond to and recover from a major incident or disaster will be based in large part upon our leadership and commitment to creating and sustaining an emergency management plan that works.

For more information about the MCC emergency management plan, feel free to contact Lee Struble, MCC director of public safety, at lstruble@monroecc.edu or (585) 292-2902.

R. Thomas Flynn is President and Lee E. Struble is Director of Public Safety at Monroe Community College, New York.

SEVEN CRITICAL TASKS

1. Establish control and communication.

2. Identify the "hot zone" (a.k.a. the "kill zone").

3. Establish the inner perimeter.

4. Establish the outer perimeter.

5. Establish the on-scene command post.

6. Establish a staging area.

7. Identify and request additional resources.

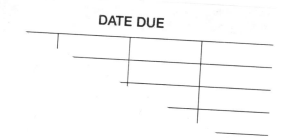

DATE DUE